THE SECRET LIFE OF
WALLANDER

THE SECRET LIFE OF
WALLANDER

An unofficial guide to the Swedish detective
taking the literary world by storm

Stafford Hildred

JOHN BLAKE

Published by John Blake Publishing Ltd,
3 Bramber Court, 2 Bramber Road,
London W14 9PB, England

www.johnblakepublishing.co.uk

First published in hardback in 2010

ISBN: 978-1-84358-248-9

British Library Cataloguing-in-Publication Data:

A catalogue record for this book is available from the British Library.

Design by www.envydesign.co.uk

Printed in Great Britain by CPI William Clowes, Beccles, NR34 7TL

1 3 5 7 9 10 8 6 4 2

Papers used by John Blake Publishing are natural, recyclable products made from wood grown in sustainable forests. The manufacturing processes conform to the environmental regulations of the country of origin.

Every attempt has been made to contact the relevant copyright-holders, but some were unobtainable. We would be grateful if the appropriate people could contact us.

To Janet, Claire and Rebecca

CONTENTS

Acknowledgements   ix

Introduction   xi

Chapter One: Henning Mankell   1

Chapter Two: Kenneth Branagh and then BBC   27

Chapter Three: *The Pyramid*   39

Chapter Four: *Faceless Killers*   75

Chapter Five: *The Dogs of Riga*   93

Chapter Six: *The White Lioness*   107

Chapter Seven: *The Man Who Smiled*   127

Chapter Eight: *Sidetracked*   157

Chapter Nine: *The Fifth Woman*   173

Chapter Ten: *One Step Behind*   201

Chapter Eleven: *Firewall*   221

Chapter Twelve: Conclusion   245

ACKNOWLEDGEMENTS

M y friend Ray Lewis, a knowledgeable enthusiast of crime fiction, first pointed out to me the strangely erratic English language publication sequence of Henning Mankell's wonderful *Wallander* novels and so provided the idea for this book. Ray also proved a great help during writing as did a great many other *Wallander* fans, some directly and many via the marvels of the internet. I was also assisted enormously by reading many other works on the subject including most helpfully: *Talking About Detective Fiction* by P.D. James, published by the Bodleian Library; Crime Fiction by John Scaggs, Routledge; The Rough Guide to *Crime Fiction* by Barry Forshaw and Ian Rankin and *The Cambridge Companion to Crime Fiction*.

The marvellous Martin Beck novels of Maj Sjowall and Per Wahloo provided an intriguing historical backdrop to the heavily populated world of Swedish crime-fighting and the wealth and quality of Scandinavian crime fiction is quite remarkable. Many magazine and newspapers have chronicled the astonishing life and career of Henning Mankell and his most famous creation and of the thousands of articles those in the *Guardian*, *The Times*, the *Los Angeles Times* and the *Observer* have been particularly helpful.

Arguments still rage over the best screen presentation of Kurt Wallander but Kenneth Branagh and the BBC have certainly done a masterful job in bringing this great character to a wider audience. John Harvey's perceptive BBC documentary *Who Is Wallander?* was also a great help to this writer.

Henning Mankell's life and humanitarian work stands as an inspiration to us all.

INTRODUCTION

When it comes to fictional detectives, either in print or on screen, you might have thought we had seen everything. After all, among hundreds of variations we've had tough detectives, poetry-writing detectives, lollipop-sucking detectives, time-travelling detectives, priest detectives, a Chinese detective, a Dutch detective, a quadriplegic detective and even a singing detective. From the pages of some of the great crime novelists we've seen intrepid investigators like Sherlock Holmes, Miss Marple, Reginald Wexford and Maigret brought to life on our screens to solve the most compelling mysteries. But in recent years, after dear old Morse expired, Rebus retired, Jane Tennison screeched her last, Barnaby finally perfected his tree impression, and Frost simply melted away, a yawning gap at the top emerged for a compelling new-crime fighter. Step forward Kenneth Branagh as the Swedish policeman Kurt Wallander, who is helping to turn writer Henning Mankell's dark and carefully crafted international best-sellers into a small screen success story.

The English-speaking Wallander first strode into action on British televisions in October 2008, as he marched into a field of bright yellow rapeseed in a desperate bid to help a terrified young girl who promptly poured petrol over her head and body and set fire to herself. It was an electrifying start to the first series of films and the excitement levels have scarcely faltered since. Kenneth Branagh's high quality version of *Wallander* is now a well-established, award-laden, audience-delighting winner and, happily, our troubled hero is going to be featuring prominently in our television schedules for years to come. Perhaps one of the most amazing things about Kurt Wallander is that it took him so long to arrive on our TVs to enthral us all.

It is more than two decades since Stockholm-born writer Henning Mankell created the small-town detective with a big-time following. In fact, it was back in May 1989 when Mankell, who was already a successful author, returned to Sweden from a lengthy spell in Africa. The passionate humanitarian was horrified by the rising xenophobia that seemed to have gripped his homeland while he had been away. Sweden had long had a proud record of warmly welcoming refugees from all over the world but Mankell detected a growing resentment against all immigrants. He wanted to write about this disturbing change in attitudes and he decided that, as xenophobia was a crime, he needed a police officer to take action. While crossword enthusiast Colin Dexter used the name of his favourite puzzle-setter for his great detective Morse, and P.D. James used the name of her English teacher for her police investigator Adam Dalgliesh, Henning Mankell was rather less sentimental. He picked the name Kurt Wallander out of the Stockholm telephone directory and drafted a dark and intriguing story about the vicious murder of an elderly couple, which is rumoured to have been carried out by 'foreigners'.

That initial *Wallander* book, *Faceless Killers*, was first published in Sweden in 1991 and became enormously popular in Scandinavia and, soon afterwards, in Germany and other countries in mainland Europe. But it was not published in Great Britain until almost ten years later. By 1998, seven further *Wallander* novels had been published, mainly in Swedish and German, and had sold more than 30 million copies all over the world. They have been translated into at least 40 different languages, including Hebrew and Chinese. The greatest success has been in Germany, where *Wallander* comfortably outsells *Harry Potter*. Unfortunately, *Wallander* initially sold much less well in Great Britain and the United States than in other countries because the books were not translated into English until much later and also because they did not emerge at the bookshops in the right order. *Wallander* is very much a developing story but British and American readers found it difficult to fully appreciate this because of the bizarre publishing policy. And European audiences have already had the chance to see more than 20 *Wallander* films with several different actors taking the lead role. Actor Rolf Lassgård is perhaps the best known Wallander on the continent, where the Swedes compare the film series to the James Bond movies and regard Lassgård as the 'Sean Connery among rivals'. But more recently Krister Henriksson has built up a significant following in Britain thanks to the BBC4 screenings of some of his *Wallander* films. His acting is certainly much more convincing than his improbable hair colour.

The action mainly takes place in and around the small Swedish seaside town of Ystad, population 17,000. In real life it is a very peaceful place where murder is an extremely rare occurrence. In fiction Mankell has brought more than 100 gruesome killings to the area and film units are an almost constant presence. The locals have learned to live with the fame *Wallander* has brought and apparently almost one-fifth of the population has appeared on screen in one film or another. Tourists come in their thousands to see the distinctive *Wallander* settings.

'I had no idea this would be the start of a long journey,' says Mankell. 'I was writing the first novel out of anger at what was happening in Sweden. The story came first, then the character. Then I realised I was creating a tool that could be used to tell stories about the situation in Sweden, and Europe, in the 1990s. The best use of that tool was to say, "What story shall I tell?" and then put him into it.'

Kurt Wallander is very far from glamorous. From the start, Mankell presents his central character as lonely, morose and socially dysfunctional. His one joy appears to be listening to opera and he has a particular affection for Maria Callas. His wife, Mona, has walked out on him and he has lost touch with their only child, a headstrong 19-year-old daughter called Linda who tried to kill herself when she was a teenager. Wallander has a difficult relationship with his ailing and cantankerous elderly father, a painter who profoundly disapproves of his son's decision to become a policeman. When he first appears, Wallander is a sleeping policeman dreaming of making passionate love to a black woman. He is not just unhappy and frustrated, he is seriously overweight thanks to the unhealthy diet of hamburgers and pizzas with which he has sustained himself since his wife departed. In a bad way physically, he has put on seven kilos in the three months since Mona walked out. Neither Mankell nor Wallander minces words and our hero berates himself angrily as a 'flabby piece of shit'.

It all sounds depressing and that is how Wallander so often feels, but he also has a shining integrity that sustains himself and his readers along with an unflagging determination to bring justice to an increasingly lawless world. Because of the brilliant way that Mankell lets us into the complex thought processes of his hero, we are with him all the way. And it is an enthralling and unforgettable journey. Seven more novels closely follow the first and Wallander plumbs the sort of depths of depression that make Inspector Morse seem like a laugh-a-minute, song-and-dance man. Wallander is lonely and unsure whether or not to remain in the police force. He knows he drinks too much whisky and eats too much unhealthy food but he does little about it. His relationship with his father is strained as the old man toils away endlessly on recreating the same landscape some 7,000 times. The symbolism of attempting to recreate a fondly remembered past is hardly subtle but it is still undeniably effective. Wallander Jnr goes on and on with more and more harrowing investigations into hideously violent crimes and becomes increasingly depressed by his life. After eight gloom-laden yet compelling books, Mankell gave *Wallander* fans something many of them desperately wanted, an insight into the young Wallander. *The Pyramid*, published in Sweden in 1999, is a collection of stories featuring Wallander as a fresh-faced young police recruit. Mankell's remarkable imagination and story-telling skills worked wonders again and the book became yet another best-seller.

As a self-confessed *Wallander* addict, I enjoyed the crime novels immensely. There was something about the unfamiliar Scandinavian background and the remarkable way Mankell somehow takes the reader with him right inside the thought processes of his flawed but fascinating detective that was absolutely irresistible. They are the sort of crime novels you never want to end because the stories are so absorbing and thought-provoking. My crime fiction-loving friend, Ray Lewis, first suggested them to me and I'm now forever grateful to him. But as I greedily gobbled up the titles as they became available in Britain, I found myself at first confused and then frustrated and deeply irritated by the peculiar English-language publishing pattern. As they appeared out of their chronological sequence, so some of the enjoyment was spoiled. For instance, *The Dogs of Riga* was bizarrely delayed, which meant that fans like myself could read about Wallander's anxiety over his ailing long-distance relationship with Latvian policeman's widow, Baiba Leipa, before we knew how he had lost his heart to her in the first place. It seemed just plain daft to me. Wallander is very much a character who develops and changes as time passes. This is very important to writer Mankell, who provides precise dates and vital references to real events as the stories unfold. In Scandinavia, Germany and most of the rest of mainland Europe the books were published in the order in which they were written and I believe this is one of the reasons why the popularity of *Wallander* grew so much faster there.

To Mankell himself the evolution of the character of Wallander is absolutely crucial. Events are all carefully rooted in relevant contemporary history and as the times move on and change, so does Wallander. Mankell says flatly and undiplomatically that he does not like detectives such as Hercule Poirot and Miss Marple, who remain static and unchanged throughout every investigation they undertake. He finds this static character state just plain unrealistic as he is convinced that everyone alters through time. He said to an American interviewer: 'When I created this Wallander character I had one ambition, which was to make him a person like you and me, someone who is always changing. I dislike these so-called heroes who are the same on page one as on page 10,000.'

The marvellous *Martin Beck* crime novels, written by husband-and-wife team Maj Sjöwall and Per Wahlöö in the

1960s and 1970s, were among the young Mankell's favourite books and he believes they have stood the test of time. Mankell has also said that John le Carré was an influence on his work and the way that George Smiley altered with great subtlety as he grew older and more experienced in each subsequent book was one of the things which appealed to him. I couldn't agree with Mankell more. People don't stay exactly the same as they go through life and it was when I was banging on about this English-language injustice that has upset me and lots of fellow *Wallander* fanatics to publisher John Blake that the idea of this book emerged. We agreed that many readers in the English-speaking world have been denied full enjoyment of the world of *Wallander* by reading them out of sequence. We decided to go through the books, examining the changing personality of this most remarkable policeman. *The Pyramid* throws much new light on the character and make-up of this, in some ways, defective detective so we have included it in what seems to be its correct timeline, before the first novel *Faceless Killers*.

We started talking about a book about the fascinating background of Henning Mankell and Kurt Wallander before it was announced that Kenneth Branagh was going to star as our hero on British television. So there it was, an excuse to wallow in *Wallander* and spend months investigating the greatest and most fascinating criminal investigator we've seen in recent times. I hope you enjoy reading it as much as I enjoyed the writing.

CHAPTER ONE:
HENNING MANKELL

Multi-millionaire thriller-writers might make their fortunes dreaming up enthralling stories of violent and shocking events like nerve-shattering gun attacks or deadly terror on the high seas but in real life they are mostly inclined to steer well clear of any genuine bullets or actual danger. Which just goes to show that Henning Mankell, the man behind Kurt Wallander, is no ordinary thriller writer. Mankell's ingeniously crafted crime stories are much more than simple money-making exercises in excitement creation. His particular police officer was created more than 20 years ago as a vehicle to explore and reveal growing injustices in Swedish society. Mankell's fiercely held humanitarian principles, which motivate the best-selling author every bit as forcefully today as at any time in his life, drove him on write a compelling series of novels that remain as thought-provoking as they are thrilling. Mankell's views have

1

scarcely softened over the years, which was why, instead of swanning around as scheduled in the warm Welsh sunshine among fellow literati at the Hay Festival on May 29 2010, he was on board a protest boat in the small flotilla carrying aid from Cyprus to Gaza, which was met in international waters with such devastating and deadly ferocity by Israeli armed forces.

Nine of Mankell's fellow activists, who were equally determined to break Israel's blockade of Gaza, were killed on board the main protest ship, the *Mavi Marmara*. Mankell did not witness the killings as he was travelling on the Swedish ship, the *Sofia*, but even there he was shocked by the violent Israeli response. He said that the soldiers who boarded the *Sofia* were very aggressive and shot an elderly man in the arm with an electric gun and another man with rubber bullets. Mankell said an Israeli soldier claimed he had discovered weapons when all he had found was a razor. 'They stole my camera, my laptop, my mobile phone, my credit cards, even my socks,' he said. Mankell was imprisoned with the rest of the protesters and accused by his interrogator of entering Israel illegally. Mankell said he replied: 'That's absurd. You brought me here.' Then the interrogator said he had read all of Mankell's books and liked them. Mankell told him they should meet in Europe and talk about it. He gave the interrogator his telephone number and said: 'I do believe dialogue is the best way.'

Mankell argues the Gaza Strip has been transformed in to the biggest open prison in the world. 'It was obvious we had to do something,' he said. 'We thought maybe we should try to break that whole blockade and the only way to do it is with a convoy of ships. When I first heard about it I thought, "It's a good idea. I'd like to be on board."' It was only when Mankell was being flown home after being deported with other protesters following a brief spell in Israeli custody that he found out that people had died in the attack. He was absolutely horrified. He believes the killings were deliberate. 'I think the Israeli military went out to commit murder,' he said flatly. Mankell is still angry at the injustice. He had previously tried to travel to Gaza and been refused entry. It is a campaign he has no intention of letting up on and he is keen to emphasise that he is against the suffering in Gaza and is not anti-Israeli. He pointed out that he has many Jewish friends and a branch of his family is Jewish. His books are widely read in Hebrew and are best-sellers in Israel. Mankell's involvement in the incident was widely reported but he said he refused to look upon himself as any kind of hero. 'The heroic people are the Palestinians, not us,' he commented. 'They have to put up with this sort of vile treatment every day.' He says: 'I was born in 1948, the same year as the establishment of the state of Israel, so this conflict has accompanied me for my entire life. For me, the thought that this conflict will exist when I die is unbearable.'

Henning Mankell was born in Stockholm into what appeared to be a very conventional middle-class family. He has an older sister, Helena, and his father was a judge while his mother helped compile the Swedish National Biography. But when Henning was a year old the family was broken up when his mother walked out. He described it thus: 'My mother did what many men do. She left.' Upset by the sudden rift, which was shocking in a society that was then deeply conservative and very formal, Mankell's father, Ivar, moved the children north to the remote and rural province of Härjedalen. He became judge in a village called Sveg, where he and Henning and Helena lived in an apartment above the courtroom. They were joined by Ivar's mother, who played a large part in helping to bring up the children.

Sveg was a very remote and chilly place. Henning Mankell's earliest memories are of deep snow and cold and darkness. 'I remember at school every June we were supposed to pick flowers and sing about spring, but it was always dark and freezing,' says Mankell. The village was surrounded by miles and miles of woods and now, years later, whenever he returns to the area he stops his car and walks a few yards into the woods, just to remember what it's like to become instantly invisible and experience total silence, 'our country's gold', as Mankell terms it. Even though they were very young, the marriage split was difficult even for the children. Helena recalled: 'At school on Mother's Day we children were supposed to write letters to our mother, but we didn't have a mother so we had to write to our grandmother instead. It made me feel a little awkward.'

Henning's grandmother was a widow and she was the person who taught him to read and write. Henning told the *Guardian* newspaper of the excitement he felt at forming his first words. 'I was six at the time,' he said. 'I can still remember the miracle that I could make a sentence, then more sentences, telling a story. The first thing I wrote was a one-page summary of *Robinson Crusoe* and I'm so sad I don't have it any more. It was the moment I became an author.' Young Henning certainly took to literature very early. He said: 'The first story that really had an impact on me and probably gave me the idea that this is what I would like to do in my life was Ernest Hemingway's *The Old Man and the Sea*. I think I was seven or eight years old when I first read it. To me that book was a miracle. The struggle the old man had with the fish, and that it was written in a way that I could see what was happening was what I remember. For every page I turned I wanted to be part of it. I wanted to sit on the old man's boat.' That joyous and almost magical feeling of being transported into another world by the flight of imagination of a simple story is something that has never left Mankell. 'It is the same feeling I get when I see really good theatre,' he enthused in a BBC documentary, *Who Is Kurt Wallander?*, about his work. 'I really, honestly believe that when I read that book it made me an author. Now I cannot imagine in my life that I ever wanted to be something else.'

Fellow thriller writer John Harvey, who wrote and presented the perceptive programme, said: 'It is an amazing image. This young, motherless boy living in a remote and isolated icy wilderness, whose life is transformed by the power of a book. The old man's struggle with the fish can be seen as symbolising man's determination to do the right thing in a troubled world.

It was clearly a huge turning point in Mankell's life and has become a common thread in his books.'

Sveg is surrounded by dark forbidding forests and the weather is often very harsh and cold but Mankell recalls his childhood very warmly. He thinks Härjedalen was a wonderful place to grow up. The court underneath the apartment was in session one day each week and Henning and Helena were under instructions to keep all noise down, though sometimes they were allowed down to watch the proceedings. Henning said: 'Naturally I got to have a great respect for the system of justice when I was very young. Every Thursday we had to be very quiet because that was the day when people were sent to jail. Sooner or later someone would come up from downstairs and ask me if they could have the use of some of my small toy cars. Then I knew it was a case where there had been an accident in cars. My father got so involved because the people could not explain what had happened so they used my cars to show it. I was very proud that they used my cars.'

On a different occasion Henning and Helena's school holidays were lengthened as their father investigated a local murder. Mankell says that ever since he was a child he has been interested in the justice system. He always had great respect and affection for his father. He remembers him as a 'kind and strong man'. Ivar was widely regarded as an excellent judge but his first love was music. The Mankell family was originally from the border region between Germany and Denmark and had moved to Sweden early in the eighteenth century. 'By profession they were musicians, church organists and violin players,' says Mankell. His grandfather, from whom he inherited his name, was a noted composer and the house was always full of music. Ivar established a concert society in Sveg in memory of his composer father, which helped to bring classical music to the distant area. Music is very important to Mankell. 'There is a melody in everything in life,' he says. 'And I honestly have learned a lot from music when I come to write.' It follows that Mankell's novels include many musical references and Kurt Wallander eases the stresses and strains of investigations with constant help from Maria Callas. Mankell himself is a fan of Charlie Parker and Verdi.

As a boy Mankell was a voracious reader. The African exploits of Scottish explorer Mungo Park became one of his firmest favourites. He found the books a revelation and used to pretend that the logs that floated down the river behind the courthouse home were crocodiles that Park encountered in the Congo. 'Africa was the most exotic place I could imagine,' says Mankell. 'It felt like the end of the world and I knew I would go there one day.' He learned very early in life of the power and potential of the imagination. As a young boy it served him well when he dealt with the absence of his mother. He told John Harvey that he did not blame his mother for walking out of the family home and abandoning him. 'I don't care because my father was a good man,' said Mankell. 'He showed a lot of emotions so I think I didn't miss anything when I grew up. But naturally I used my imagination to create a sort of mother to replace the one who had gone.' This imaginary mother, he says, helped him through this 'crisis of life' and his sense of isolation. 'I did meet my real mother when I was 15 years old,' he says, 'and, maybe this sounds brutal, very quickly I realised I preferred the mother I had created in my mind for myself. Obviously then I realised that imagination is a tool that is enormously important in life.' Mankell told one interviewer that when he met his mother in a restaurant in Stockholm aged 15, her first words to him after all that time were: 'I have the flu.'

Before then, when Mankell was 13, his father moved his family south to the town of Boras, near Gothenburg. Mankell attended the local secondary school but quickly became bored and frustrated by the rigid curriculum. He did not shine academically and left school aged 16 determined to become a merchant seaman and see the world. His father was disappointed yet supportive. He did sympathise with his son's restless spirit and did not stand in his way when he rejected the idea of university or any other form of further education. Young Henning worked as a stevedore on a Swedish ship, which carried coal and iron ore to Europe and America. He got on well with almost all of his shipmates, describing them later as 'decent and hard working', and was delighted to become part of a tightly knit community on board. Later he said his time as a teenage merchant seaman was his 'real university', which was every bit as beneficial to him as a conventional seat of learning would have been. He enthused over this period in his life and insists: 'It was a romantic escape which was my dream. I loved some of it but there were long boring times as well.' Although Kurt Wallander took his time to visit Britain, his creator travelled to Middlesbrough 25 times.

After two years at sea he moved to live in Paris in 1966, at a time when the city was the focus of much political unrest. Mankell was a wide-eyed 18-year-old drinking in the exotic experiences of student activism. He absorbed many challenging ideas and experienced some serious personal hardships. With hardly enough money to live on he often went to bed hungry. 'I still don't know how I survived, but I did,' he said. After an exhilarating and hugely educational 18 months, he returned to Sweden determined to carve out a career in the precarious world of theatre. By the time he turned 20 Mankell had got himself a job as a stagehand in Stockholm and written his first play. It was called *The Amusement Park* and was about Swedish colonial involvement in South America in the nineteenth century. It was relatively well received but Mankell himself has decided: 'It was not very good.'

The process of writing, however, was already deeply ingrained in the young man. He was desperately saddened when his beloved father Ivar died in 1972, just before Mankell had his first novel, *The Stone Blaster*, published. The book tells the story of an old man looking back on his life and about the need for solidarity between people in Sweden. Mankell remains proud of the novel which is still in print in his home country, though it has not yet been translated into English. Although his father did not live long enough to see his son's book in print, Mankell says he knows that his father always believed in him and knew that he would one day have success as a writer.

The childhood dream of one day going to live in Africa was still very much alive in Mankell and by the winter of 1972 he had somehow saved enough money from his meagre wages as a stagehand to make it come true. He travelled first to Guinea-Bissau on the west coast, which was then still a Portuguese colony. Later he said: 'I don't know why but when I got off the aeroplane in Africa I had a curious feeling of coming home.' Mankell visited different parts of Africa and lived for a while in Zambia before moving to Mozambique where, in 1986, he was invited to run the Teatro Avenida in the capital, Maputo. His arrival in Mozambique was like something out of one of his novels. The country was then torn by civil war and Mankell's plane crash-landed to the accompanying sound of gunfire. His time in Africa often sounds idyllic but the early days establishing the Avenida were desperately difficult. There was no real tradition of theatre in Mozambique so in many ways Mankell was forced to start virtually from scratch. It was very important to Mankell to spend time away from Europe. He said he wanted to build himself a 'tower' outside of his home continent. 'In Africa it was like when you're a hunter and you build towers to watch the animals move. I knew I would never understand the world without that perspective. I came to Africa for that rational reason, although I love Mozambique now. You can have more than one home. You can carry your roots with you and decide where they grow.'

Mankell always declines to discuss his private life in detail but it is clear he has enjoyed a good deal more success in his relationships with women than Wallander has ever managed. At any rate, although he is now happily married to Eva, Mankell has four sons (Thomas, Marius, Morten and Jon) from what are described as 'previous relationships'. He married Eva in 1988 when he was 50. She is the daughter of Ingmar Bergman and his second wife, the dancer Ellen Lundstrom, and is a choreographer and theatre director. She has directed several of her husband's plays.

Early in 1989 Mankell returned to Sweden after a long spell away and he was deeply shocked by how much his homeland had changed. The assassination of the Prime Minister and leader of the Swedish Social Democratic Party, Olof Palme, in 1986 had already had a huge impact on the mood of the nation. Palme and his wife, Lisbet, were walking home from the cinema, as usual without any security guards, when a man who had been following them pulled out a gun and shot them both. Palme died but his wife recovered. The killer disappeared into the night and although a man was later convicted, the conviction was overturned. He was released and the crime remains one of the greatest unsolved mysteries in Swedish history. Mankell was, like millions of Swedes, absolutely devastated by the murder and by the disastrous police investigation which followed. Palme was seen as the father of the Swedish nation, the man who had stood up against America's war in Vietnam and against apartheid in South Africa. Left-leaning Mankell regarded Palme's killing as a terrible crime. For Swedes it was as shattering as President Kennedy's assassination was for America. Mortified by the murder, Mankell said: 'The trauma is that it never became solved and that we have to live. I don't think it will ever be solved.'

Mankell was also particularly horrified by the increase, during the years he had been in Africa, in racism in the homeland he had always felt to be such a liberal country. There had been a series of vicious neo-fascist attacks on immigrants that decided Mankell to write about this sickening new development. 'Racism is a crime, I thought,' he said. 'So I'll use a crime story. Then I realised I needed a police officer.' Having plucked the name Wallander at random out of the telephone directory, he added: 'I know it was May 20, 1989, when Kurt was born because I looked it up in an old diary later.' That first *Wallander* novel, *Faceless Killers*, was published in 1991. It opens with a savage murder of an elderly couple and the dying wife mouths the word 'foreigners' just before she breathes her last. Once that gets out to the general public, more hideous violence erupts and Wallander finds himself struggling to contain an alarming outbreak of violence. It is a shocking and deeply disturbing book in many ways, which is exactly what the author intended. It succeeded in getting the writer's point across that angry attitudes of racial hatred are both mindless and abhorrent.

But it was also a cracking crime novel. As a character Wallander was instantly compelling, especially to his countryfolk and to readers in the rest of Scandinavia,

Germany and much of northern Europe. 'I work in an old tradition that goes back to the ancient Greeks,' says Mankell. 'You hold a mirror to crime to see what's happening in society. I could never write a crime story just for the sake of it, because I always want to talk about certain things in society.' He considers the best crime story he has ever read is *Macbeth* and says: 'It is a terrible allegory about the corrupting tendency of power that could equally be about President Nixon or Stalin.'

Mankell ingeniously devised his intrepid investigator to be personally flawed but professionally dedicated. Almost nothing else really matters to Wallander apart from solving the latest crime. He has allowed his marriage to disintegrate, lost touch with his only daughter and become frequently at odds with his eccentric elderly father. He tries to do his best for his family but often fails while he gives absolutely everything to his job and always gets his man in the end. To me it is the extraordinary level of detail that Mankell includes about Wallander's astonishing thought processes that mark him out as different. Certainly there have been plenty of detectives with personal problems before. Hercule Poirot is always painfully fussy and a hypochondriac to boot, while Sherlock Holmes was a cocaine addict with the unnerving habit of firing his revolver at the wall when he was bored. But Mankell recounts the level of Wallander's thought processes so intimately that the reader can almost feel the mood swings of the dedicated detective.

Not only that, the stark landscape of southern Sweden

around the seaside town of Ystad where Wallander lives and works is also eloquently evoked. And the often harsh and unforgiving weather that is familiar to the district of Skåne, which surrounds Ystad, is equally brilliantly described. Fellow writer, A. N. Wilson, eulogised about Mankell's writing in the *Daily Telegraph*: 'The bleak weather, the featureless but haunting rocky fields are so well evoked they form movies in our heads.' Another voice worth listening to was that of Ruth Rendell who explained that, quite apart from their other strengths, the *Wallander* stories are 'landscape novels' firmly based in Baltic geography. She said: 'I don't think English readers realise just how important landscape and natural history are to Swedes.' We scarcely comprehend the impact of those long cold dark winters, she felt, and went on: 'I mean, spring is almost an ecstatic event to them.' Rendell, who is half Swedish, considered the books have a 'dream-like' landscape that is recognisably Baltic but could be almost anywhere else in northern Europe. 'I find this very potent,' she wrote. 'There is a belief that crime fiction should be about little old ladies solving murders in country villages, but Mankell is modern and he makes you reflect on today's society.'

The Dogs of Riga soon followed *Faceless Killers* but it was not until the third *Wallander* book, *The White Lioness*, was published in 1993 that the detective's stories began to climb the best-seller lists. It is set partly in South Africa and involves a sinister plot to assassinate Nelson Mandela and derail the dismantling of apartheid. Impressively, the writing fully lived up to the ambitious scale of the novel and the book was published in several Scandinavian and European countries at the same time, leading to sales figures going through the roof.

In Britain and America, where the books were delayed in translation and published out of order – even though they were carefully written in a strictly chronological sequence – sales were understandably much slower. As Nick Hasted put it in the *Guardian* at the start of 2002: 'Henning Mankell's novels about Swedish police inspector Kurt Wallander have spread like wildfire across Europe, but the first sparks have only recently begun to burn in this country.' All nine *Wallander* books came out in Sweden before the fourth was published in Britain, but there were some influential folk in among the early fans in this country. Apparently former Prime Minister Tony Blair was a great *Wallander* enthusiast and at least half his cabinet loyally followed suit.

Some observers believe that the American market will always be difficult. Steven Murray, the Albuquerque-based translator of several *Wallander* titles, says: 'There is not enough wham-bam stuff or violent shoot-outs for the Americans.' He might have something there but for this reader the action is always more than adequate and the great appeal is to see the long and complex procedures gradually leading us to the ultimate deduction and arrival of justice.

It was an especially disappointing start in Britain, where there has long been a widespread enthusiasm for detective fiction from Scandinavia. Danish writer Peter Høeg's unforgettable *Miss Smilla's Feeling for Snow* is generally credited with helping to push open the door for crime thrillers from chillier climates and writers like Karin Fossum and Eva-Marie Liffner have joined Mankell on the bookshelves of Britain, as well as the late Stieg Larsson, whose *Millennium* trilogy has sold millions worldwide. All of these writers must have been at least partly inspired by the brilliant *Martin Beck* books of Maj Sjöwall and Per Wahlöö, which stylishly covered some similar ground in the 1960s.

In Sweden the nine-book *Wallander* series was completed as long ago as 1999. There should have been a tenth book but as Mankell explains: 'I was halfway through writing one more *Wallander* story when I stopped and burned it. It was more than ten years ago. I had written 150 pages and then I just felt that I couldn't go on writing it. The subject was too bad, too evil, it was a book about the abuse of children. It will never appear though obviously today I regret burning it. I feel a bit ashamed of my actions because I should have written it because child abuse is a horrendous problem in the world.'

Mankell says that there are many parts of the *Wallander* stories that have been difficult to write and people ask him where he gets all his morbid ideas from. 'I always say that whatever I write, the reality is much worse,' he says. 'I can never in my wildest imagination find things that are worse than what is carried out in reality. That is my defence.' He points out that he started *Before the Frost* with a story about someone who pours petrol on swans and sets them on fire and the poor creatures are seen flying along and at the same time burning alive. 'People asked me how I could invent such a horrific thing,' says Mankell, 'and I replied that I saw it in a newspaper! It had happened.' In fact, *Before the Frost* was published in 2002 and it is not strictly a Kurt Wallander novel as his daughter, Linda, takes over at the centre of the action. After taking a long time to decide on a career, Mankell has strong-willed Linda following him into the police force. In the story it is Linda's best friend from childhood who disappears and leads her into a gripping mystery involving a religious doomsday cult that starts with the burning swans. Swedish actress Johanna Sällström played Linda Wallander in a film of *Before the Frost* and the character was later developed and seen investigating alongside her father in a series of TV films, which have been screened on BBC4 in Britain. Even with subtitles, they were enormously enjoyable and Sällström's stunning presence and fine acting ability added much to the successful production. Sadly though, Sällström suffered from severe mental problems and committed suicide in February 2007. She had recently been released from a psychiatric unit where she had been having treatment for depression. The actress and her one-year-old daughter had been traumatised by being caught in the 2004 Indian Ocean tsunami. They were in Thailand and almost drowned together in the catastrophe. They survived only because Sällström was able to hold onto a tree with one hand and her daughter with the other. The suicide shocked Sweden, where she was very popular, and completely devastated Henning

Mankell. Readers remembered that the teenage fictional Linda had herself survived a suicide attempt. Mankell was unable to even contemplate writing the two further novels he had planned with Linda taking over from Kurt as the central character. The writer said that his grief was simply too great. He explained at the time that he had decided to retire his detective: 'I did it out of respect for myself and my readers,' he said. 'I did not want them to feel I was bored.'

Mankell did gradually build up a considerable following in Britain and his fifth *Wallander* novel, *Sidetracked*, won the Crime Writers' Association Gold Dagger for Fiction in 2001. Writer and legal commentator Marcel Berlins shrewdly pointed out: 'If you think about it, these Scandinavian whodunits are really quite British. Of course there is something new and strange in them for Anglo-Saxon readers, but they're also curiously, comfortingly familiar. The morose and grumpy Wallander is a sort of Baltic Inspector Rebus and the flat, monotonous landscapes in these euro-thrillers remind one of Norfolk.' Most *Wallander* stories are hardly whodunits for long. Generally the excitement builds towards the climax of the investigation even though Wallander and the readers know full well the identity of the killer. Novelist Maggie Gee is a devoted fan: 'I am seduced by the leisurely, layered craft with which Mankell establishes the humanity of his policemen, not just Wallander, but his supporting cast of shambolic squad members, through their colds and stomach aches, their cheap cars which break down when they need them, their failing eyesight and needy families.' She finds the long and intense stories have the 'density and pleasurable authority of a nineteenth-century novel'.

The author's fame grew steadily and, since completing the *Wallander* series, Mankell has written some 13 other novels and a number of plays. A self-confessed workaholic, he insists: 'When I stop writing I will die. For me creativity is the lifeline of my own life. The day I lose my creativity I will not survive for very long. In a very non-sentimental way, that's my life.' He seems uninterested in wealth for its own sake and uses the large amounts of money that *Wallander*'s international success generates largely to help the people of Africa. He says that Africa has taught him that the worst thing in the world is so much suffering that is absolutely unnecessary. He believes mankind could stop much of it tomorrow if we had the will. He says: 'No child need die from malaria. How much do you think it would cost to teach every child in the world to read and write? Lots of money, yes. The same lots of money that we in the West spend on pet food!' He gave more than £1 million recently for the construction of three villages and a school for orphan children in Mozambique. He also financially supports the fight against Aids in Africa, and the Memory Books project which is particularly close to his heart. Parents who are dying from Aids are helped and encouraged to write and draw pictures about their lives as a record for their children, and to leave behind a message for future times. Mankell is passionate as he explains: 'Books are messengers, like the *Diary of Anne*

Frank, they speak for the dead. The Memory Books will be the most dramatic books of our time, the heritage of being human. Aids is the most catastrophic disease in the history of mankind. It is killing off complete societies. There will be herds of kids without parents.' As John Harvey elegantly described Mankell's work in his TV documentary: 'That small boy in Sweden who created a mother in his imagination now enables hundreds of children to keep their mothers alive in their imagination.'

Mankell continues to live part of the year in Africa and part of the year in Europe. He says he has 'one foot in the sand and the other in the snow'. He says it is a complete life rather than a double life. 'I am like an artist who must stand close to the canvas to paint, but then stand back to see what he has painted. My life has that movement. Some things you can only see at a distance.' He thinks his African experience has made him a better European as he has learned so much about the human condition by living in Africa. He tries to live as simply as he can. 'I have a small apartment in Maputo. I have an old car,' he says. His home in Sweden he says is 'wonderful but not very big'. He steers clear of the trappings of affluence because he says: 'Then I can use the money for good thing and that is what I do. I am happy to be able to do that.' The idea of buying Rolls Royces and yachts does not appeal to him. 'I do not understand greedy people,' he says. 'I never have and I never will. I just don't understand what they are thinking of.' Mankell today remains as prolific as ever. The dream he pursues in his sixties is the same one he has had since he was six when his grandmother taught him how to read and write. 'All I have ever wanted to be is a storyteller,' he says.

Mankell can pinpoint the moment when he realised that the character of Kurt Wallander had really registered with the reading public. 'It was in 1994,' he says, 'and in Sweden we were having elections to see if we wanted to be members of the European Union. I was walking up the main street in Stockholm and a man about my own age came up and said, 'Excuse me, I recognise you and I know who you are. I have a very important question for you.' Then he asked if Kurt Wallander was going to vote "Yes" or "No" to the European Union. I gave him an answer, which was that he would probably vote the opposite way to which I will vote, and then I left quickly.' Mankell was surprised but pleased that to his readers his troubled creation was becoming a real person. He said: 'I realise that people see Kurt Wallander like one of themselves, and that is important to me.'

He insists that although he and Wallander are the same age, they are two very different people. 'We share a love of music and a Calvinist attitude to work. I am a very hard taskmaster,' he says. 'But otherwise we are not too similar and I don't like him too much.' Mankell's friend and publisher, Dan Israel, points out that if Wallander were left-wing and very progressive in his political views, as Mankell is, then the thrillers would most certainly not be nearly so popular. 'Really, Wallander is a kind of spokesman for the worries of the common man,' says Israel. 'Henning has an uncanny ability to decipher the signs of the times. He knows how to tap into people's fears and uncertainties.'

Mankell is careful to make sure Kurt Wallander is no kind of police superman. He is vulnerable, fallible and at all times very human. His readers seem to relate to this realistic portrayal. In fact, when Mankell wrote in an illness his popularity rating went up. 'I realise that people see Wallander like one of themselves,' says Mankell. 'I call it the diabetes syndrome. After the first three novels I asked a female doctor friend, "What kind of disease would you give this guy?"' With Wallander's massive workload and complete inability to eat healthily or get enough sleep, there was only one answer and it came instantly. 'She said immediately, "The way he is living, diabetes." So I gave him diabetes and that made him even more popular.'

Mankell chose to base *Wallander* in scenic Ystad, a small and outwardly peaceful coastal town with a population of some 17,000, for a reason. At the end of the 1980s, when he returned to Sweden after some time in Africa, he was shocked to find that problems of drugs and other social evils were no longer confined to the big cities. 'Before, if people wanted to buy drugs they had to go Stockholm or Copenhagen,' said Mankell. 'But that had changed and I was sorry to discover that it was possible to buy any kind of drugs in Ystad. That is why I chose a small city to show that when it comes to social problems there is no difference where you live. The second reason I based *Wallander* in Ystad is that this part of Sweden, the region called Skåne, is like the Texas of

Sweden. It is border country. We are on the coast here and 200 kilometres away across the sea is Poland and the rest of Europe. This kind of border town has a special kind of dynamism that I wanted to use.'

The success of the *Wallander* books has had a huge impact on Ystad. Tourists flock from all over the world to see the places they have read about in the novels. They can stand and stare at the windows of their hero's bachelor flat on Mariagatan, eat enormous *Wallander* cakes at Fridolfs Konditori, which is his favourite café, and at the Hotel Continental you can even reserve Wallander's private table so your can eat your lunch in your hero's favourite setting. The bartenders in Ystad all seem to know that Wallander enjoys Glenmorangie single malt Scotch whisky. Later, you can drive out to view the wide and beautiful landscapes, which give all of the screen versions of the stories such remarkably distinctive atmosphere, and track down as many horrific murder scenes as your stomach will stand.

Ystad used to have an actual policeman by the name of Inspector Kurt-Ingvar Wald and the similarity of the name meant that he was often approached for his autograph. 'The entire Ystad police force has read the *Wallander* books,' said one-time Chief Inspector, Kent Persson. He thought that, while sometimes they were a little 'exaggerated', it was: 'A stroke of genius to set them in Skåne.' As he put it: 'Skåne is closer to Poland than Stockholm and criminals from the Baltic States have brought in drugs from across the sea.' More recently, a female Ystad Detective Inspector called Ewa-Gun

Westford gave the *Wallander* series her personal seal of approval when she said she had read all the books and identified very strongly with their hero. 'Yes he is a real good police officer,' she said. 'But first of all he is a good human being, very tender and caring. I don't think he is very proud of himself.' Ewa-Gun clearly feels Wallander's heart is in the right place and his low self-esteem makes him more attractive. But she concluded sadly: 'I don't think Kurt thinks he is a very sexy man. He has too many things to think about before sex, so by the time it come to that he is very tired.' She also agrees with Mankell that Ystad has some serious criminal problems. 'Of course there is a dark side to life in Ystad,' she said. 'We have had some problems with young people drinking too much alcohol and others beating their women up and some problems with drugs coming in from Poland and other parts of Europe. Social problems are coming closer and closer because the city of Malmö is not very far away.' But while Wallander's total death count is now well over 100, the actual murder rate in Ystad is mercifully not too exceptional. 'Since the year 2000 we have had seven murders here,' said Inspector Westford. Not too terrible, you might think, but as she added quickly: 'It is seven too many.'

Mankell accepts the bizarre elements of the public reaction with a good grace. 'I have a very childish view on all that,' he says. 'After all, Sherlock Holmes still gets letters to 221b Baker Street and I love that. One of the spin-offs is that Ystad will get new friends. I like the idea that people think that Wallander is really alive, like the man who wanted to know how he would vote. *Wallander* is sold in 120 countries now and translated into more than 40 languages. How on earth is he popular in Korea? I still believe it is because he is a man who keeps changing and is always dealing with his inner demons.' Mankell sees Wallander as being like his 'brother in arms', as the character definitely appears to have developed a distinct identity of his own. The writer says it is easier for him to say what he will not do, than what he will do. 'He will never become a cynic,' says Mankell. 'For me, that is the most scary thing to think about becoming. Sometimes I meet people who I once liked and find that particular man or woman has become a cynic. I think it is worse than if they had become an alcoholic. I will never become a cynic.'

Mankell believes that Wallander's sacrificial life is a key part of his appeal. It reveals just how difficult it is to be a good police officer. Real policemen and women often thank Mankell for showing the enormous strain the job places on their lives. Of course, Wallander is damaged by all the effort he puts in but his obsession for getting to the bottom of every investigation is what drives him on in life. As Mankell puts it: 'If he didn't do the work he would feel worse. He would leave a big black hole in himself. I think he is of the Calvinist generation, in the sense that you are supposed to work and pray while you are sweating. That is supposed to be your life.'

CHAPTER TWO:

KENNETH BRANAGH AND THE BBC

Many of the millions of readers who enjoy Mankell's captivating novels featuring the stressed Swedish detective Kurt Wallander were concerned when they heard that he was to be played on television by Kenneth Branagh. The acclaimed English actor has a remarkable track record of fine performances but he was hardly anyone's mental image of the overweight, overworked, desperately dedicated policeman from the little town of Ystad that they had come to know and love. Some of us worried that the new screen *Wallander* might be glamorous and slick, with the essential humanity of our hero lost in the mind-numbing task of converting a series of deliciously dense 500-page books into 90 minutes of entertaining television time.

But we need not have concerned ourselves. Kenneth Branagh is just as big a fan of *Wallander* as any of us and he was not about to lend his star quality to anything that did not do its level best to do justice to the compelling Scandinavian stories. As Kenneth Branagh said at the outset: 'Wallander is a wonderfully complex and compelling character, and as a long time admirer of Henning Mankell's novels, I am very excited to be playing this fascinatingly flawed but deeply human detective.'

Happily for all concerned, particularly the viewers, Branagh really was a genuine fan of the *Wallander* novels. 'I read them purely for pleasure,' he said. 'My first experience of these books, their stories and characters was entirely as a member of the public, enjoying these rip-roaring tales and great whodunits. The world that Wallander lives in is a raw world where people have to deal with terrible news and the death of loved ones in terrible circumstances. Wallander is very self-aware, perceptive and intelligent about human behaviour. For me this is more of a straight part as Wallander's character does not have all the same eccentricities that would normally appear in these types of stories.'

Branagh said that his interest in *Wallander* was started by reading the first book, *Faceless Killers*, and he was, 'pretty much hooked' right away. 'It had some kind of X factor, a quality of place and atmosphere and such a compelling central character that meant I couldn't put it down,' he said. 'I read them all in a space of about a month, I think. It was a delicious period of steeping myself in the character and the place. It is tough for him because he does love the job that he does. It gives him certain advantages in the battle of life and certain disadvantages. Seeing him try to resolve those is very rewarding dramatically.'

Some observers might think that the very driven, obsessive personality of Wallander is eccentric enough. Branagh and the producers wisely stripped down the Wallander character from the books to its essentials. Music plays a huge part in the life of the Wallander of the novels, and indeed in the life of Mankell. But while readers are used to Wallander turning to Maria Callas in moments of stress, the screen detective is apparently no great opera fan. A BBC executive told me quietly that this was because it might have made him seem too much like a copy of *Inspector Morse*. Certainly, it is the level of success and critical acclaim achieved by ITV with John Thaw's brilliant portrayal of Colin Dexter's cerebral Oxford-based sleuth that the producers would love to emulate. But while the Morse of Dexter's books was fundamentally changed in his transformation to television, somehow the Wallander in our minds from the novels is not so very different from the permanently unshaven and haunted-looking Branagh. In the novels Wallander drives a series of aged Peugeots which have a habit of letting him down until he can negotiate a loan to buy a newer model. This motoring quirk was removed from the screen Wallander, who drives a dull but deeply efficient Volvo.

'I think that partly what made the books so successful was that readers could experience the stories through Wallander's view of the world,' said the actor, before the series of films had been screened. 'I believe Rick Cottan's script captures this and allows the viewers to become part of how Wallander reacts to what he is seeing and I think this will make the television series very compelling. There is a responsibility to try to do something as well as you can and with such a fine writer as Henning Mankell, we really wanted to do it justice. Everyone involved already loved the books and the responsibility to get it right was keenly felt by all.'

Branagh was determined to capture Wallander's sensitivity that is such an important characteristic of the books. 'I believe the scripts reveal the constant questioning in Wallander's mind and show his on-going empathy. There is an open wound quality about him.' The production team wanted to show that for the police and anyone involved in the discovery of these violent crimes, the horror of it all is very far from usual. They never become hardened or insensitive to the suffering they see. 'I have a sense that particularly in some TV procedural drama there is a sort of "Oh, it's another killing" feeling,' says Branagh. 'There is a kind of weariness and over familiarity with death that creeps in. With Wallander it costs him and his colleagues emotionally each time, so there is no getting used to it.'

Branagh was determined that *Wallander* would be different, a television event rather than just another new cop show. 'I hope that we deliver very compelling stories that make you want to watch from the word go,' he said. 'I hope that we deliver images which are unusual that are born out of being in another country and in another kind of atmosphere. I think that most we wanted to capture the balance that Henning Mankell strikes in his books between telling a great story of a police procedural tale with the sensitivity and substance of being a human being.' Branagh feels passionately that Wallander is a thinking and feeling man whose thoughts are 'much closer to the surface' than they are in other people. The actor says: 'He has questions about his place in the world and about his relationships that we all have.' The peculiar difference of course is the way that he deals with them. As Branagh notes: 'His gifts for dealing with people seem to be placed entirely at the disposal of his work, rather than with dealing with his own life.'

The Swedish setting is crucial to the novels as the bleakness of the landscape and the extremes of the weather often become integral parts of the stories, and Branagh and the production team were keen to capture that on television. 'When you read the novels it makes you want to come here to Sweden to have a sense of whether that unease you're describing and seeing in the settings is genuine,' said Branagh. 'It is absolutely right that we came to shoot in Sweden as they have a different relationship to the landscape. People are much more aware of what the environment can do to you and Sweden has the kind of atmosphere that is a really good place for drama.'

Swedes are sometimes characterised as being cold and detached but Branagh was delighted to find they were delivering to the screen people who were exactly the opposite. His Wallander simply seethes with emotion as the camera lingers on him. Branagh wanted to show a man who is tremendously sensitive to the workings of the human mind. 'It is a great gift as a policeman and as an investigating officer,' he said. 'But it also costs him enormously as it exhausts him spiritually and emotionally, and often physically as well. It makes a tremendous amount of sense that his capacity for empathy and using his gifts as a human being seem to be placed entirely at the disposal of his work and is much less effective in dealing with his own life. If he could use the same degree of sensitivity and perception and intelligence that he is able to employ when it comes to the analysis of a witness or a piece of evidence on his relationship with his daughter or on finding out why his marriage has not worked, then life might be very different for him.' Branagh loves the way that Wallander is able to constantly question everything about his life and believes that Swedes are perhaps naturally more able to examine and re-examine issues in a way that might be considered embarrassing in Britain.

'Wallander is fascinating to play,' said Branagh. 'He feels very, very alive to me and I am enjoying getting to know him in this sort of three-dimensional version. He has a lack of vanity and a very open quality about his character that is very appealing. His daily struggle to be a better human being is very moving.' Branagh pointed out to Mankell when they met for a promotional interview for the series that he was impressed by the extremely tight time frames of the stories. Mankell spells out in detail in his books many of the precise times and dates of particular events. Branagh said as they were making the films: 'It always amazes me that such extraordinary events happen in such a few days and during that time Wallander might have fallen for someone or made some connection... my heart goes out to him as he finds a chance of romance. I find his openness very beguiling. He is just trying to be the best person he can be from moment to moment in a very, very flawed way.'

Mankell's firm conviction that Wallander must never become cynical about life is fully taken on board by Branagh and the creative team. Branagh says there is a 'nice moment' at the end of the film of *Firewall* where Wallander talks to his daughter Linda about meeting the woman from the dating agency she arranged. 'It doesn't work out,' says Branagh, 'but he tells Linda she was right to do it and says, "I thought I was dead inside. I'm not, I'm still alive."'

Wallander is a far from perfect policeman. In the books he breaks into suspects' homes, slaps them during interrogations and has been caught drink-driving and let off by colleagues who turned a blind eye. He is desperately lonely after his wife walks out on him and is often drawn to the most unsuitable women. He makes a pass at a young married prosecutor and deeply regrets it afterwards. He makes mistakes, strays far too often into danger and has a habit of ignoring correct police procedure. He eats too much, drinks too much, doesn't sleep enough, battles depression and diabetes, and is constantly promising and failing to turn over a new leaf.

In spite of all that he is totally determined to solve every crime he comes across and is constantly appalled by the rising tide of anti-social behaviour and violent crime that he believes is swamping Swedish society. Successful crime writer John Harvey, presenter of the BBC documentary *Who Is Kurt Wallander?*, says: 'What I like most about the character is that he just never gives up. Dogged, that's the word. When he is involved in a case you know he is going to carry it through, however dangerous, until it's sorted and solved.'

On screen, Kenneth Branagh and the production team have worked hard to recreate this complex yet captivating character, who has enthralled and delighted so many millions of readers. Perhaps the single most memorable screen image came from the shocking opening of the first of the BBC films, *Sidetracked*, when a terrified young girl set fire to herself in a field of yellow rapeseed as Wallander/Branagh desperately ran to try to help her. Philip Martin, who directed that film and *One Step Behind*, is understandably enthusiastic about the end result and has his own particular take on the films. 'The detective Kurt Wallander is a cranky, complicated, damaged, anti-social, internalised person, so is not someone the audience would immediately connect with. I think that Kenneth Branagh has given the character such humanity and such tenderness that you care what happens to him. He has been able to show how the things that are happening in Wallander's personal world and the crime story are totally intertwined. As a director you are always trying to achieve something new... I think we have given people a very magical world that has got its own logic but at the same time is very relaxing to watch.'

Relaxing is not quite how I'd have described them, but they are thoroughly enjoyable all the same. Philip Martin's great skill has certainly delivered some sensational story-telling, and he has fully taken on board many of the ideas behind Mankell's remarkable work. Martin has used the foreign location to provide British viewers with something they certainly welcomed, a crime series with a very different angle. The setting may look very different from what we're used to yet it all seems believable and real.

Martin said: 'I felt that a big part of the *Wallander* stories is the perceived collapse and failure of the '60s and '70s to deliver the Utopia it promised. The books are set in a time when people thought that the world could be changed. People thought that good architecture, a good liberal democracy, a good civic pride and a sense of corporate responsibility would deliver a better world.' Many of the social problems Mankell saw in Sweden in the '80s and '90s also exist in Britain. There were, however, some important differences which had to be overcome. As director Martin pointed out: 'A fundamental part of British cop drama is when the cops kick the doors in. Unfortunately part of the wonderful Swedish health and safety laws mean that none of the doors in Sweden open inwards. They all open outwards.' So that's why Wallander and his team are never seen booting open people's front doors.

Sidetracked swept away to a highly successful start on

screen with 6.2 million viewers, a quarter of the total, switching on to see Branagh's Wallander struggling to solve the mystery of a horrific double murder at a remote farmhouse. The reviews were very good. In *The Times*, Andrew Billen enthused: 'This distinctly superior cop show is both spare and suggestive, and brilliantly acted.'

Wallander went on to win six British Academy of Film and Television Awards, including Best Drama Series, while Branagh won the Best Actor prize for the title role at the Broadcasting Press Guild Awards. After it was screened in the United States on PBS in 2009, it was nominated for two Emmy awards. The three films quickly became an international success with some 14 countries, from Canada to Finland and from Slovenia to Australia, buying the drama. In the bookshops sales of the three adapted titles quadrupled within weeks.

Branagh in particular was heartened by the warm public response and was happy to return to the role for three more films. 'I'm delighted to be back in Kurt Wallander's shoes for three further adaptations,' he said. 'The character's story becomes ever more complex in these films. Our entire team relished the privilege of bringing them to the screen, and to an audience who proved so loyal last time out.' Branagh was overjoyed by the positive public reaction: 'The reaction to the first series was fantastic. I think the audience responded well to the pace and the atmosphere of *Wallander*. I think they liked being given time to think. I think they enjoy Wallander's grumpiness.' Branagh felt that the audience enjoyed the experience of being taken to a foreign location, somewhere that looked and felt very different, for a crime series. He promised that the new series would take the chance to go a little deeper into the minds of all the characters, not just Kurt Wallander. 'And it keeps us very much on our toes,' added Branagh. 'We will go even deeper into the minds and psychologies of the characters in the second series, particularly of course Wallander, but also the other people in the police station, from whom he often seems quite distanced.'

One of the other popular faces in the *Wallander* line-up is that of Tom Hiddleston, who plays the bright but occasionally impulsive younger police officer, Martinsson. He was particularly delighted to return to Sweden to make three more films. 'When you know that it's been received well you're not worried about, "Is it going to work?" So you can almost relax into it more and that means you can go further and deeper into your character.' In his case it means the 'latent antagonism' between Martinsson and Wallander can be explored further.

Also the two women, Sarah Smart and Sadie Shimmin as Ann-Britt Höglund and Lisa Holgersson, become larger characters. 'The value that Höglund has to Wallander is very important,' says Branagh. 'They are both fine actresses and they get a little more chance to show it in the second three films.'

Real-life Ystad policewoman Ewa-Gun Westford was one of the biggest fans of the series. She said: 'I think the BBC has done an excellent job with the *Wallander* films. When I first saw it on the screen I thought, "Oh wow! Is the sky so blue or the fields so green?" I think you came from another country and you saw Sweden with new eyes. I think it is excellent.'

CHAPTER THREE:
THE PYRAMID

Kurt Wallander first came into the world in the book *Faceless Killers* in 1991. He was then aged 42 and it was set in January 1990, just two months after the fall of the Berlin Wall that heralded so many extraordinary changes in European society. The brave and highly principled policeman from the small Swedish seaside town of Ystad went on to become an international success story as Henning Mankell's series of compelling crime thrillers attracted millions of devoted fans.

But Mankell realised many readers were keen to know more about this professionally brilliant yet domestically disastrous man. The writer was enthused by the avalanche of fan mail from *Wallander* followers who wanted to learn of the formative years of their favourite detective and he put together a collection of five short stories called *The Pyramid*, from the time before the Iron Curtain was drawn back. And Wallander as a young man turned out to be every bit as enthralling as the older, world-weary guy we've all come to know and love.

The Pyramid was published in Sweden in 1999, after eight previous novels follow the adventures of the middle-aged police detective. But we include it before our look at those eight books because it features stories with events involving Wallander as a young policeman.

WALLANDER'S FIRST CASE

Wallander's First Case recalls the time when, aged 21 in 1969 and still a very inexperienced young policeman in Malmö, he was stabbed by a stranger. The story starts with Wallander in the early days of his relationship with Mona, the woman who is later to become his wife. Mankell reveals that Wallander first falls for Mona on the rebound from a relationship with a girl called Helena, who dumped him. Mona is a young woman who works as a hairdresser and dreams of one day having her own salon. She never sounds like the most exciting woman imaginable. She was sitting knitting on the ferry from Copenhagen when they met. But Mona certainly inspires some degree of sexual excitement in Wallander, as Mankell discretely describes. He writes: 'Wallander noticed he was becoming very excited at the very thought [of a night with Mona]. He straightened his trousers and then crossed the street...'

Wallander's relationship with his painter father is exciting in a very different way. Previously, when Kurt told his father he was going to join the police force the old man was so angry and upset that he almost disowned his son. Wallander Snr was sitting in his studio when Kurt broke the news and it could hardly have gone down any worse. He hurled a brush at his son and told him he never wanted to see him again. But Kurt was determined. He had made his mind up that he wanted to become a policeman and he stuck firmly to his guns. His father eventually calmed down a little but from then on there was a huge rift between the two men. Kurt's mother died young, while he was training to be a police officer. The childhood home was anything but happy once Kurt had made his controversial career choice and his sister, Kristina, was sensible enough to move out as soon as she was old enough to go and live in Stockholm. Kurt moves into a one-bedroom flat in an old building in the Rosengard area of Malmö while his father decides to move away to Österlen to live in the countryside. Kurt has no security about the future of his home as the building is listed for demolition.

Wallander's First Case shows Kurt struggling with his role as a uniformed officer. After police roughly handle some left-wing demonstrators protesting against the war in Vietnam, he feels a backlash from his sneering father, who supports the cause of the protesters. His father is enraged and accuses Kurt of beating innocent children over the head with a stick. Wallander furiously insists he has never hit a single person in his entire life but his father is not listening.

Serious crime comes to Wallander very early in his career, when he discovers his neighbour lying dead on the floor of his living room with a revolver next to his hand. Wallander calls the police station and detectives quickly take over. Inspector Hemberg instantly challenges Wallander's suggestion that his neighbour has committed suicide. But Wallander sees the mysterious sudden death as an opportunity to fulfil a long held ambition to become a detective himself and he starts to make his own investigation. That doesn't go down well with Mona when he becomes distracted by work and forgets he is supposed to be meeting her.

The plot thickens when Wallander's neighbour's apartment is mysteriously broken into and then set on fire. Hemberg encourages Wallander to use his local knowledge and position on the spot to help with the investigation, and challenges him to come up with ideas of what might have happened. Then to the surprise of the police, the autopsy on the dead neighbour reveals that he has some valuable diamonds in his stomach. Wallander works hard to find out as much as he can about the background of the murdered man, but still finds time to have another furious row with his difficult and unpredictable father. Wallander vows never again to bother to try and repair their disastrous relationship. His investigation takes a grisly turn as he checks on his late neighbour's last movements and finds another corpse, a woman with a bicycle chain tightened around her neck!

Hemberg is impressed by Wallander's results but furious that he has gone off on his own without reference to anyone else. Hemberg angrily tells Wallander there is no room in police work for individuals going off secretly, following up leads without telling any other members of the team. Wallander nods that he understands but, of course, this is something he will be guilty of repeatedly doing in the future. One of the great attractions of Wallander is his stimulating directness of approach. As his fans know so well, he is always prepared to go off on his own on a complete tangent to everyone else. Hemberg, who could surely never imagine his orders were falling on such deaf ears, advises Wallander to remember everything he has seen in great detail and evaluate all possibilities in the search for a clue. This is advice that Wallander clearly does take on board. He is fighting to launch his career in this investigation and although he is naïve and awkward, his enthusiasm and intelligence shine through. Hemberg sees potential in the ambitious young policeman. He makes Wallander examine every detail he noticed at the scene of the woman's murder. Wallander realises he is being given an important test and desperately tries to make his early deductions as perceptive as possible. 'You have to use your eyes,' says Hemberg. Wallander passes the test but, as so often, his chaotic personal life arrives to interrupt his police work.

Kurt's sister, Kristina, arrives and takes him to task for not visiting his father's new house out in the countryside at Löderup. She accuses him of pretending he doesn't know his father when he sees him looking scruffy and confused in the street. She says their father is very upset with him. Wallander is annoyed. His father has not been telling the truth; he did not even tell his son he was moving, let alone where to. Eventually, when he is helping him to pack, Wallander drops an old plate and that sparks a furious row between the two men. Kristina begins to see his point of view but Wallander has more trouble when Mona suspects he is still seeing previous girlfriend Helena. Mona takes shock action and slaps Wallander hard across the face before storming off. He is hardly left in the mood for meticulous investigation but somehow he struggles to get his mind back on the job.

In this later work, Mankell allows himself the freedom of more occasional humorous asides than in the earlier novels. One of Wallander's colleagues reports dryly: 'The nearest neighbours gave the impression of being regular Swedish citizens. That is to say, extremely nosy.' Wallander seems to realise that this investigation is his big chance of becoming a detective and he ploughs on relentlessly. He discovers that his dead neighbour has changed his name and the real identity unlocks details of a murky past in South America that eventually lead to a successful arrest.

It is not an easy journey however. Wallander interviews one potentially key witness over a meal of mussels, which react very badly with his digestive system. He spends the night, as Mankell puts it, 'shitting and vomiting'. Hemberg advises him to drink plenty of liquids but is still keen to hear of the latest developments. Wallander, still officially a uniformed officer, has to break off trying to be a detective to patrol the streets, which is a job he hates. But after he goes off duty and is out for a walk in his own clothes, he is recognised in the park in Malmö by one of the anti-Vietnam demonstrators. A girl yells that he is one of the cops who assaulted her and a man lunges with a knife. Wallander is stabbed in the middle of his chest and he sinks to the ground unconscious. He is very close to losing his life and stays out cold for four days. He has to undergo two complex operations. The knife has grazed his heart. When he wakes on the fifth day Wallander has no idea that he almost died but he is delighted when he opens his eyes and the first face he sees is that of his girlfriend, Mona. This attack is to haunt Wallander in the future. The girl's angry hatred for the police in general and himself in particular is harder to deal with than the physical attack. Her utter contempt for him, the representative of the forces of law and order, is chilling to Wallander. It signifies a fundamental change of attitude throughout Swedish society that frightens him.

After he has recovered and received the go ahead to return to work, Hemberg visits him in his apartment and tells him how the case was concluded. Wallander's discovery that the dead neighbour had changed his name proved crucial as it provided the essential link to the man who killed him. Hemberg explains that his neighbour had swallowed the diamonds and killed himself so the murderer could not steal them. The murderer went on to kill the neighbour's former lover as he thought she knew where the jewels were. 'It was just a horrible little murder,' says Hemberg, with the benefit of his years of experience. Hemberg told Wallander that he had made many mistakes as he doggedly attempted to solve the crime. He should never investigate alone and he should never go into dangerous areas without back-up. But he commends Wallander's stubborn determination that had helped bring the case to a successful conclusion. Wallander is overjoyed when Hemberg tells him that he will be moving from the uniform branch of the police to the criminal investigation department, which is his greatest wish come true. He strokes the scar on his chest and recalls a quotation he had once read. 'There is a time to live, and a time to die.' He decides this will be his motto from then on. Mona arrives and they happily plan their trip to Denmark. But deep down Wallander knows that it is his career move that has lifted his heart even more than his love for Mona.

THE MAN WITH THE MASK

Kurt Wallander next appears in a shocking short story set on Christmas Eve 1975. Readers learn quickly that much has changed for the young detective. He and Mona are now married and have a five-year-old daughter called Linda. They have decided to move away from Malmö as next summer Wallander is to transfer to a new job in Ystad, some 35 miles away on the south coast. He and Mona have already moved there to an apartment in Mariagatan, in the middle of town. Wallander knows perfectly well that moving from a major city to a small town is unlikely to advance his career, but he feels a need for change and Mona is able to buy a hair salon in Ystad for a knockdown price. Wallander already knows some of the detectives at Ystad with whom he will be working and has struck up a friendship with a middle-aged policeman called Rydberg. The widely held view of Inspector Rydberg within the force is that he is rude and difficult to get to know or like, although he is undoubtedly very good at his job. Wallander does not find Rydberg's somewhat abrupt manner at all off-putting and he is very impressed by his professionalism. He thinks he can learn a lot from Rydberg.

Wallander is commuting to work and looking forward to a week's holiday after his last shift on Christmas Eve. He rings Mona to say he is about to leave, only for her to interrupt by asking harshly if he is ringing to say that he is going to be late. Wallander is irritated by this response. He and Mona have never exactly been love's young dream and five years of marriage have resulted in a relationship that seems full of difficult and unhappy moments. Wallander lets his irritation show as he explains that he is in fact ringing to say he is on his way home. As he replaces the receiver, he reflects sadly that he and Mona do not even seem to be able to have the simplest conversation without acrimony. Mona never misses any opportunity to nag me and she probably feels that I do the same to her, he thinks, glumly. He knows that without their little daughter, Linda, they would be even further apart. The child is holding the marriage together, he thinks.

Husband and wife are often at loggerheads and do not seem to be able to agree on anything. Mona wants her husband to leave the police force and get a better paid job with more regular hours with a security firm. Wallander still thinks he can become a good policeman and build a successful career in the force. He does not want to leave but he realises that Mona is at least partly motivated by the potential danger of his current job. She knows he would be much safer working for a private security firm. Moving to Ystad is something of a compromise for the two of them though, of course, if Mona really believes that Wallander's life in Ystad is likely to be safe and peaceful then she is certain to be disappointed.

Wallander's boss in the squad is Inspector Hemberg, the officer who had such faith in him as a rookie uniformed cop with ambitions to join the detectives. It is Christmas Eve and Wallander has his coat on and his car keys in his hand when Hemberg asks him to take a look in on the way home to check on a woman who runs a grocery shop and who has telephoned to report a suspicious character hanging around outside. It is in the direction of Ystad and Hemberg tells Wallander to call in and wish her a Happy Christmas on his drive. It is raining heavily as Wallander steps through the door of the shop. As soon as he gets inside he feels that something is wrong. There is no one around and the shop is silent. He calls out for the owner, then opens a door to another room and sees a woman lying face down, a pool of blood beside her. Then suddenly he sees a figure looming from behind him and he is knocked out cold.

Wallander wakes to find his arms and legs tied up with what he realises is the tow rope from his own car. The place is still silent and Wallander struggles to free himself.

He is shocked by the sight of what he realises is probably. the body of the murdered shop owner. He can't conceive how an old woman could be so cruelly killed in her own shop on Christmas Eve. Then he sees a man, wearing over his head a black hood with two slits for eyeholes, holding what looks like a metal pipe. The man says nothing and just stares at Wallander and then checks to see that he is still securely tied up. Wallander struggles to understand the situation. He can't work out why the man stands there staring at him. He knows that if he doesn't arrive at home, then at some time his wife Mona will raise the alarm, but he can't count on anything happening very soon. His reputation for last minute unreliability should see to that. The man in the mask leaves Wallander's view as mysteriously as he had arrived and Wallander struggles to get to his feet, his arms and legs still tied to one of the shelves in the shop. But as he peers over the counter he sees the man in the mask standing with his back to him. Wallander lunges towards the man but then sees that he is holding a gun, which, alarmingly, is pointed straight in the direction of Wallander's head. Wallander is convinced that his life is about to end, tackling an intruder in a typically meaningless robbery that has somehow got horrendously out of hand.

Wallander pleads with the man not to shoot, and explains that he has a five-year-old daughter. Wallander thinks the man is keeping him in the shop because he has seen the body of the woman, whom he presumably killed. Wallander tries to talk his way out but there is no response from the man in the mask. Wallander decides he must be out of his mind, but no less dangerous for that. The phone rings but the man makes no move to answer it. Wallander attempts to take charge of the situation and tells the man he is a policeman and orders him to put the gun down. The man still does not respond and then takes his mask off. Wallander is confronted by a wild-looking black man. Wallander repeats what he has just said, but in English and he sees that the man understands what he is saying. Wallander warns the man that more policemen will arrive very quickly and the best thing to do is to give himself up now. Eventually the man speaks and tells Wallander that his name is Oliver and he comes from South Africa. Wallander tries to sympathise about the way black people were badly treated under the apartheid system. Oliver seems unimpressed and tells Wallander chillingly: 'I can kill you.'

Wallander tries to engage with Oliver and asks him about life in South Africa. Oliver says his father was beaten to death by the police with a hammer when the only thing he had done was to join the African National Congress. Oliver himself is now on the run from the South African authorities. He says if he is captured he will be killed. Wallander attempts to convince Oliver that the police in Sweden are very different, that he will be treated correctly, but that he must give himself up. Suddenly, Wallander hears the sound of cars braking outside and of car doors opening and closing. He knows the cavalry has arrived but that it might be just too late as Oliver still has the gun. Wallander shouts to Hemberg and his men outside to wait. Then Oliver fires a shot into the roof. Wallander grabs him and the two men fight. Oliver kicks Wallander in the stomach and points the gun at him again. Wallander is convinced he is going to be shot dead and he closes his eyes. A shot rings out and Wallander looks to see a shattering end to the story.

It takes Wallander a long time to recover anything approaching his composure. He rings Mona to tell her he has been delayed, but on the advice of Hemberg he doesn't tell her everything in detail until later.

THE MAN ON THE BEACH

Kurt Wallander is significantly older as the next story in *The Pyramid* collection begins, a fact neatly illustrated as we first encounter our hero snipping hair from within one of his nostrils. It is April 1987 and the policeman is now almost 40-years-old. His years of hard and intuitive investigative work have resulted in him being promoted to the dizzy heights of Detective Chief Inspector.

Unusually his desk is extremely neat and tidy. There has been a lull in crime fighting and his wife, Mona, and daughter, Linda, have just flown off on holiday together to the Canary Islands. Wallander uses the sudden bonus of spare time on his hands to clear his desk, which is normally a complete mess. The holiday for his womenfolk came as a complete surprise to Wallander. He hadn't known that Mona and Linda were planning to go away together and he didn't understand how Mona had been able to get enough money together to pay for it.

Linda has been uncharacteristically secretive lately. She is growing more independent as she grows older and has recently refused to stay on at grammar school in spite of her father's strong views about the importance of education. Wallander had been baffled at first but he soon came round to the idea of Mona and Linda going off together.

He quite fancies the prospect of a couple of weeks on his own. He knows that his marriage is in trouble as communication with Mona has become more and more difficult over recent years. Wallander knows that it is really only the presence of Linda that is keeping him and his wife together. He realises Linda will be wanting to move away sooner or later and in his heart he doubts if he and Mona will stay together after that.

As if that was not depressing enough, he is putting on weight as his wife is quick to point out. He has started to look more than his age, which is another thing to upset him. It almost seems as if an intriguing murder mystery is just what Kurt Wallander needs and, of course, one arrives right on cue. A taxi driver turns up at Ystad police station deeply disturbed that a passenger in his cab has finished up dead at the end of a journey. The driver says he thought the man was just ill and rushed him to the hospital but he was already dead when they arrived.

Wallander quickly discovers that the deceased had been a successful businessman who had recently taken to walking along the beach every day. At first the doctors suggest it is death from natural causes as there is no sign of any violence or injury to the man. Wallander gets

Hansson on the case and the officer finds out that the dead man was divorced ten years previously and that his only child, a son, died in some sort of accident seven years earlier. He has been on holiday near Ystad and Wallander and Hansson rush to check his hotel room to see if anything there can throw light on the mystery. The room yields nothing useful but conversations with local taxi cab companies reveal that the man had visited the beach several times recently. Then comes the shock news from the medical-legal department in Lund that the man had died from poisoning. Either he had taken the poison deliberately in order to commit suicide or someone had killed him.

At first there are no leads to go on at all. Wallander is told that the dead man used to walk on the beautiful nearby beach every day. Hansson digs into the death of the man's son and discovers there was some evidence to support his father's strong opinion that his son was murdered but no one was ever charged with the crime. Wallander has the man's ex-wife tracked down and finds out that she got a divorce because she found their marriage was so boring. Wallander does not consider boredom to be a good enough reason to cast adrift another human being, someone you have once loved. Wallander thinks he will ask Mona, when she returns, if boredom was the stumbling point in their marriage. The murder couple's son was beaten up in a motiveless assault in a Stockholm street five years earlier and sadly never recovered from his injuries.

Wallander draws a blank with his inquiries until he

begins to look into the officials responsible for dropping the investigation into the boy's death. He gets very angry when information is not provided quickly enough and says: 'You should know by now that my patience is more or less non-existent.' When a lady prosecutor who had made the final decision is discovered to live close to the beach where the poisoned man was seen walking, the hunt closes in on the killer. But there are still some enthralling surprises before the case is finally closed.

THE DEATH OF THE PHOTOGRAPHER

Kurt Wallander married Mona at the end of May 1970 and to mark the occasion she insisted they had some suitably atmospheric photographs taken down by the beach near the Saltsjobadens Hotel in Ystad. Wallander thought the allegedly 'romantic' result was not worth the money that was paid to Simon Lamberg, a successful and now affluent local photographer.

But when Wallander receives an early morning call from Martinsson almost exactly 18 years later to alert him to the fact that the snapper has been brutally murdered, at least the detective has a clear recollection of the unfortunate victim. In his hurry to get to the murder scene as quickly as possible he skips his normal shower but still finds time to brush his teeth, which produces a wince of pain as he touches a damaged tooth that produces a moment or two of agony. He reflects as he leaves the house that Simon Lamberg had not been around to record the occasion around a month previously when Mona had announced she wanted them to separate 'for a while'. She said then that she wanted time to think about their future. Wallander was unprepared for the speech but not surprised by the message as he knew that he and his wife had grown further and further apart in recent weeks and months. Wallander had pleaded with Mona not to leave but she was adamant she was returning to Malmö to live, and worse still she was taking Linda with her.

Wallander struggles to wrench his mind off his personal disappointments and get it back onto the job in hand, which is the murdered photographer. Although he has been his subject several times, Wallander finds it difficult recalling anything remotely distinctive about Simon Lamberg as a human being. The corpse in the photographer's own studio is certainly not a pretty sight. Wallander finds the body lying with a pool of blood all around the dead man's head. Eerily, the man's eyes are still wide open. He had been smashed hard on the back of the head. Martinsson is surprised when Wallander orders that Svedberg goes to break the dreadful news to Lamberg's widow. Martinsson feels Wallander should do the uncomfortable job himself and says so.

Still suffering badly from his painful tooth, Wallander starts his investigation by interviewing Lamberg's cleaner, who found the body. She says she hardly knew her employer and once the conversation is concluded Wallander rushes off to the dentist to have his broken tooth dealt with. As a boy he was terrified of going to the dentist but somehow he has overcome his childhood fears and now simply wants the problem dealt with as swiftly as possible. When the treatment is over he races back to the investigation. As he returns to the scene of the crime, he briefly reflects on his boyhood ambition to become a photographer. Not a man with his own studio like Lamberg but a press photographer who would always be on hand to record all the great events. It was a dream that had soon deserted him and he swiftly returns to the matter in hand, the search for clues in Simon Lamberg's studio. When keys to the drawers are produced there is an extraordinary find. Hideously distorted photographs of famous people, showing them looking misshapen and deformed into loathsome monsters, are discovered in the bottom drawer. Wallander wonders why a photographer famous for portraying people at their very best should seek to hoard such appalling images. Then Svedberg points out a particularly gruesome image and says to Wallander: 'That's you!'

The sight of his own photo presented in such a ghastly fashion really shocks Wallander. He is no stranger to hatred and even abuse from some of the people he has arrested over the years. But the fact that someone he did not know was so keen to deface and degrade his photograph makes him feel increasingly uncomfortable. Wallander is outraged to be included in this macabre collection and says so. Later he interviews Lamberg's widow and discovers that they have a seriously handicapped daughter called Matilda, who lives in an institution. She says that although they were still married, she and Lamberg were no longer close. That night

Wallander gets a tip-off that someone has entered the studio again. He rushes over and gets a glimpse of a shadowy figure running out of the building. Wallander gives chase and gets knocked out cold for his efforts. His assailant gets away and the police can find nothing taken or evidence of tampering inside the studio.

This story shows Wallander experiencing a roller-coaster of emotions as potential leads crop up and are then swiftly discounted. But when a local resident hands in a hymn book which appears to have been dropped by the man who assaulted Wallander, it takes another enthralling turn. Wallander concludes that the hymn book is just the latest mysterious factor in a case he fears he might never solve. He is totally captivated by the investigation. It seems as if the only time he misses Mona is when the laundry piles up so high that he has to deal with it himself.

Lamberg's widow says that her husband's personality changed after he had been on a bus trip to Austria some seven years earlier. But they lived such separate lives that she did not know what was going on inside his head. That rings a bell with Wallander, who is still wondering ruefully what sparked Mona to leave him. Is he really so boring? If she had not taken Linda with her, he thinks he might have been able to bear it more easily. Linda might have been wilful and difficult at times but Wallander had felt they were still close.

The police follow up a rumour that the dead photographer might perhaps have been a big time gambler, in trouble because of the size of his secret losses.

57

Wallander travels to Malmö to pick the brains of an old contact from the world of high stakes betting, who operates on the very fringes of legality. Svedberg uses his initiative and visits the mental institution where poor Matilda was a patient. He learns that while Lamberg's widow visited every week, her husband has never been near the place, despite his apparent devastation at his daughter's sad condition. But Svedberg also says that there was another woman who visited Matilda, whose identity was unknown. Wallander heads for the institution to inquire about the mystery woman. He is offered the chance to meet Matilda, who is blind as well as mentally handicapped, but he rejects it. At this point, Mankell slips in the fascinating information that it is 'almost impossible' for Wallander to confront the seriously handicapped. Another intriguing facet of the complex character of the dogged detective is revealed.

Of course, persistence is one of Wallander's most important qualities. He refuses to be beaten and goes relentlessly from one chink of a lead to another. In the search for the killer of Lamberg, he goes next to talk to the driver of a bus trip to Austria some years previously. Lamberg's widow said that her husband went on the trip without her and returned a completely changed man. Wallander wonders if there is some key to Lamberg's death in what happened on the holiday. Svedberg has tracked down the driver, who has now retired, and who, conveniently and a shade improbably, keeps a record of all the passengers he drove on trips. He even has photographs of this one and provides

Wallander with the fascinating information that Lamberg began a relationship with the wife of a vicar while enjoying the delights of the Tyrol. The driver knows that this was likely to spell trouble as the vicar was himself on the bus trip. The vicar's wife subsequently died of cancer of the liver and told her husband on her deathbed of her infidelity.

The night before Wallander is to meet the man whom he believes could be a vital part of the investigation, the detective is hit by a wave of sadness at home. He misses his wife and daughter and fights off the urge to make an emotional telephone call to them. In the early hours of the morning he boils a couple of eggs and eats them standing in front of the sink. It is a picture of a man who is able to function on his own, but only just. He needs a good woman to love but he fails ever to invest the time or energy in taking care of any partner. Wallander appears to understand and accept that he is married to his job, though he would perhaps never openly articulate the feeling.

Wallander and Martinsson find the vicar in his church and Wallander feels this is a job he should take on alone, so he tells his junior colleague to wait outside. When he sees the vicar looking deeply emotional he begins to wonder if this was the correct decision. The vicar snarls that he is grieving and demands to be left in peace. Wallander instantly thinks the vicar is slightly unhinged and he is left in no doubt when the man savagely attacks him. Wallander realises this is the man who knocked him out near the photographer's studio.

They have a spectacular fight which ends when the detective manages to grab a candelabrum, which makes an effective weapon.

Afterwards it becomes clear that the vicar was not in his right mind after his wife confessed to having the affair with Lamberg. The vicar loved his wife very deeply and was completely unhinged by the news she had cheated. He began to blame Lamberg for his wife's death and started stalking him and eventually brutally murdered him.

Wallander and his colleague conclude afterwards that Lamberg was a pretty vile sort of character. The distorted and mutated photographs he had crafted are seen as a spiteful, small-minded man's attempt to get even with more successful people.

Wallander is still puzzled by the vicar's wife spending time visiting poor Matilda. He says again quietly at the end of this compelling story that there are 'secret rooms' in many people's minds that no one can enter. Hansson simply thinks Lamberg was crazy. But wise old Rydberg suggests that Swedish society is beginning to leave people feeling so powerless and insignificant that they no longer take part in ordinary interchanges. Instead they invent strange rites for getting their point across or their emotions out. Rydberg says glumly that if that really is the case then, 'our nation is in trouble'. Wallander sadly agrees and adds: 'The foundation has really started to crack.' After successfully solving another brilliantly crafted case he feels tired and a little despondent. And he misses Mona.

THE PYRAMID

The Pyramid opens with the fatal crash of a light aeroplane in a remote area of southern Sweden early on the morning of 11 December 1989. The pilot and his only passenger are both killed on impact as the plane hits the ground. The plane's secret mission and the double death lead Wallander into another enthralling mystery.

Before news of the crash reaches him, the policeman is still emotionally very raw as it is just two months since his wife Mona left him for good. He is day dreaming idly of leaving his flat in central Ystad and moving to the country, to somewhere, as Mankell put it somewhat unromantically, where: 'He can walk straight outside in the morning and piss on the grass.' Wallander wants to get a dog but decides he ought to move first. And deep down he is still refusing to admit to himself that his marriage is over. He wants to get Mona back but he hasn't the remotest idea of how to achieve that. News of the crash soon pushes personal thoughts from his head and Wallander and Martinsson head off to investigate the crash. Just as they are leaving the police station Rydberg walks in, looking dreadful. He tells them to go on ahead and they both notice how ill he is looking. Wallander feels a pang of concern as Rydberg is his closest friend in the force. In fact he is possibly his only friend in the force.

Wallander's original mentor in the police was Inspector Hemberg in Malmö but we learn that he has died in a traffic accident the previous year. Wallander makes it a personal rule never to attend funerals but he broke it to go to Hemberg's ceremony. Since Hemberg has gone, the enigmatic older officer, Rydberg, has become Wallander's role model at Ystad. After years of working together, he regards Rydberg as the most skilful criminal investigator he knows and realises he is still learning from the deep-thinking and experienced policeman. But Rydberg suffers badly from rheumatism and lives on his own. In his darker moments Wallander wonders if that is how he will end his own days, as a lonely old man with nothing to worry about apart from his ailments. He thinks: 'I've just turned 42. Will I end up like Rydberg?'

The plane crash proves a puzzle. The police find that the aircraft's markings have been obscured and they know that the men who lost their lives must have been up to no good. Illegal narcotics are coming into Ystad and the whole region of Skåne in unprecedented volumes and they realise this flight might have had something to do with the booming trade. Wallander is dwelling on this problem as he returns to the station to interview a suspected drug dealer. He is convinced the man is guilty but aware that he has not got enough clear-cut evidence to mount a successful charge against him. Raids on the man's operation were badly coordinated and somehow the dealer had been tipped off. The police arrived to find all traces of drugs carefully removed from the scene.

Wallander is forced to release the man but as he does so, he cannot resist telling him that he knows he is involved in extensive drug trafficking in the area and that sooner or later the police will find the evidence to put him behind bars. The man's lawyer, who 'resembles a weasel', notes Mankell, protests that this sort of threat is against the law. Wallander cheerfully agrees and challenges the lawyer to have him arrested. Wallander is clearly very angry that he is powerless to take any action. He reflects with great irritation that the drug dealer will walk free and drugs will continue to flood into the area. Wallander sadly knows that this is a battle the police can never win. He believes the only possible hope is that future generations of young people reject drugs completely.

His thoughts are interrupted by an angry call from his father, upset that Wallander failed to come round the previous night as they had arranged. Wallander knows there was no such agreement but his father accuses him of being forgetful and suggests his son use a police notepad to write down his appointments. Wallander wants to correct his father but he is too busy to argue and meekly agrees to go round that night. He is annoyed that his father's emotional blackmail always seems to bring results. Wallander's family certainly continue to play on his mind. He considers calling his ex-wife, Mona, to talk to his wayward daughter Linda. As Mankell puts it: 'She is 19 and a little lost.' She has recently returned to the old idea of upholstering furniture as a career but Wallander knows she is likely to change course many more times before she settles down.

Wallander might have brilliant insights but he is certainly not a policeman who never makes mistakes. He realises he has not asked the drug dealer about the crashed plane, if only to see his reaction. He does, at least, remember to visit his father. Although it is a fractious and often difficult relationship, Wallander still experiences a feeling of tenderness when he arrives. He knows that once his father dies he will be the next to go. They play poker even though Wallander's father accuses his son of cheating. Wallander Snr also has a surprise for his son. He announces he is going to take a trip to Egypt, to see the Sphinx and the pyramids. He says time is running out and it is something he wants to do before he dies. Wallander is shocked by the news. He thought it was Italy his father wanted to visit. He can't believe the old man has really thought the idea through. But it seems he is serious as he tells his son that he is flying direct to Cairo by Egypt Air and he has booked a hotel. His father waves the tickets proudly and Wallander has to believe he is telling the truth.

He is flying to Egypt in three days time. Wallander tries hard to talk his father out of the trip. He suggests he delays it until either he or his sister can go with his father but that suggestion is flatly rejected. Wallander is exasperated and tells his father he is almost 80 years old, which is too old to do that sort of thing. But Wallander's father refuses to budge and eventually his son realises that there is nothing he can do to stop the trip. Although his father's mind seems to occasionally play tricks on him, his health is generally good for his age and he has been blessed with a strong and indomitable spirit. So Wallander accepts that the trip will happen and offers to take his father to Malmö on the first leg of his epic journey.

As he drives away from yet another disturbing and surprising evening, Wallander accepts that he has a strange father. But the old man seems perfectly happy in himself and seems to experience none of the dreaded loneliness of old age which so frightens Wallander for his own future. The old man still paints the same picture over and over again, just as he did when Wallander was a child. He appears to simply ignore old age and Wallander wonders if in the end that might not be such a bad policy. On a practical level Wallander's father has neglected to take out any travel insurance so his son arranges cover.

Not that Wallander's only emotional problem at this stage is his father. He is also locked into an increasingly unsatisfying relationship with a lady called Emma Lundin, who is a nurse at Ystad hospital. They had met at the post office, struck up a conversation, and after only two days launched into a highly physical affair. Wallander appears somewhat ungallantly underwhelmed by the bedroom side of the relationship. Emma is a year younger than he is and is divorced with three children. Wallander realises that she feels more for him than he does for her and decides to end it. He knows that he wants someone who will be able to replace Mona in his heart, which poor Emma cannot do. In fact he knows he really wants Mona back, however impossible that might be. He is still jealous that Mona has a new man in her life, even though they are divorced. He decides to end the fling with Emma but he bottles out of breaking the news.

In fact, the next time Emma rings, just as she is leaving

work at around seven o'clock, Wallander is undecided about what to say. He isn't sure if he wants to see her again but he asks if she wants to call in. He knows this will mean they will go to bed together so he rushes upstairs and changes the sheets. Emma is small with brown hair and beautiful eyes but Wallander would rather be sleeping with his ex-wife. He and Emma drink wine and listen to music and at around eleven they go to bed, with Wallander still thinking of his ex-wife. They both fall asleep afterwards. Later she gets up to go home and Wallander pretends to be asleep. Then he thinks more about Mona and feels worse about the way he is treating Emma. He realises he cannot go on like this much longer. The two months since Mona finally left him feel like two years.

That night there is an emergency callout. Wallander arrives at the scene of a fire in a sewing shop run by two elderly sisters. The women are later found dead, but they have each been killed with a bullet to the back of the head rather than in the fire. A double murder of two apparently innocent old ladies shocks even the hardened detectives. Wallander can't comprehend how anyone could do such a thing as killing 'honourable old ladies'. But Rydberg observes thoughtfully that this is the point at which they should begin, by checking to make sure they really were 'as honourable' as everyone seems to think. Wallander is very surprised by this thought but Rydberg simply smiles and warns against jumping to conclusions too quickly.

Wallander's father is certainly an interesting character.

When the detective arrives early in the morning to take his father to Malmö he finds the old man sitting on his case in his driveway waiting. Wallander Snr is wearing a suit and an aged pith helmet for his trip. When Linda meets them in Malmö to see her grandfather off, she compliments him on his fine hat. Wallander is relieved she herself is dressed more conventionally than often the case. He also realises that she may have inherited her rather unorthodox dress sense from her grandfather. The two of them seem very close these days, thinks Wallander. As the old man chugs away on the ferry towards Copenhagen airport, Linda says she hopes she will be like her grandfather when she reaches his age. Wallander groans inwardly. Growing to be ever more like his father is one of his own personal nightmares.

Wallander is dazzled by his own daughter. She is not conventionally beautiful he decides, as he studies her while they have breakfast together at the Central Station restaurant but she is strikingly confident and independent, and currently besotted by the idea of a career in furniture restoration. Wallander feels a little inadequate when Linda says it's a pity neither he nor Mona is wealthy enough to pay for her to go to France to study. Wallander offers to take out a loan but Linda says wisely that loans have to be paid back. Wallander's spirits lift when Linda criticises Mona's new boyfriend for reading comic books. He asks his daughter to come and live with him but she says living in Ystad would drive her crazy because it's so small.

Linda soon turns questioner and asks her father why

he doesn't find himself another woman. He keeps quiet about Emma. Linda suggests he advertises but Wallander says he would simply find himself with someone he didn't get on with. But Linda persists and shocks her father when she says that he needs 'someone to sleep with'. Wallander is horrified. Linda has never spoken like this to him before and he finds himself telling her about his relationship with Emma. They part as friends but Wallander is left wondering about his strange family: a father flying off alone to Egypt and a daughter with her feet very firmly on the ground.

He soon comes down to earth when he gets back to the police station. His bone-headed boss, Bjork, angrily criticises Wallander for taking time off for personal reasons while he is in charge of a murder investigation. Wallander is incandescent with rage and tells Bjork he is most certainly not 'going to take any shit' from him. Wallander has put in so much extra work on investigations that he can't believe he is being hauled over the coals just for a quick drive down the road to Malmö. And he is keen to know which of his colleagues squealed to Bjork about the trip.

Wallander investigates the elderly sisters and discovers they had much more money than it seemed they could ever have earned from the sewing shop. They also have a lavish house in Spain and Wallander starts to wonder if they are involved in the lucrative business of dealing drugs. But before he can develop this theme, there comes a personal shock – his friend and colleague Rydberg suddenly collapses at work. All the officers are upset but

Wallander is absolutely devastated. Rydberg is his closest friend and he is shattered. He tries to be professional and continue with the investigation but his biggest problem is compensating for the absence of Rydberg. So often the sick officer was the man whose brain provided the key breakthrough. With him slowly recovering in hospital Wallander realises the onus is on himself to come up with the inspirational lateral thinking.

And just when Wallander thinks nothing else can surprise him, he receives astonishing information from the Ministry of Foreign Affairs in Stockholm. Martinsson hands Wallander a telex that knocks him sideways. It tells him that his father has been arrested in Cairo and accused of 'unlawful entry and forbidden ascent'. He is due in court and is clearly in serious trouble. Wallander is stunned to learn his father attempted to climb the Cheops Pyramid, which is very clearly against the law in Egypt. To his horror, Wallander realises that there is no alternative for it. He has to fly to Egypt and get his father out of jail. At first he cannot believe he must break off investigating a plane crash and a gruesome double murder to fly off and rescue his father. He heads home in something of a daze and drinks two large tumblers full of whisky before reading the telex again just to make sure it was not a joke. But no, it was real. Still bewildered, he phones his daughter Linda and asks her advice. The response is instant and exactly what he expects; he must go to Egypt. Next day, fortified by more alcohol, he is on board a flight to Cairo where his elderly and increasingly demented father is being held behind bars. Luckily for his father, Wallander has a large amount of cash, which he has just borrowed to buy a new car.

In the chaotic hustle and bustle of Cairo, Wallander is greatly helped by an Egyptian policeman called Radwan, who explains that his father is in trouble for breaking strict laws. But when he finally gets to see his father in his cell, the old man is not in the least surprised to see him. Instead he is outraged at his treatment and insists he wants to protest to the highest authorities that people are prevented from climbing the pyramids. In fact he is quite happy to serve out his expected two year sentence until Wallander explains that he will probably not be allowed to paint in prison. Wallander can't understand why his father wanted to climb the pyramid but he is touched by the explanation. 'It's a dream I've had all these years,' says his father. 'I think one should be faithful to one's dreams.' Wallander realises he has to get his father out. He is so old and frail that Wallander is desperately concerned that if he is sent to prison for any length of time, then he will die. Later he returns to his hotel and then takes a walk to look at the pyramids for himself. He is overwhelmed by the size of them and he begins to understand his father. We should be faithful to our dreams, he thinks. And he considers how faithful he has been to his own.

Common sense prevails in court next day as Wallander pays the fine and gets his father out of jail. Later the old man insists on taking his son to see more of the pyramids and the Sphinx. Wallander is amazed at how much his father knows about these ancient structures. But as

Wallander plans his trip home next day, his father insists on staying for the rest of his booked holiday. He does promise to keep out of trouble and eventually thanks his son for flying across the world to rescue him. 'Next time we'll go to Italy,' promises his father.

The first thing Wallander does when he returns to Ystad is to ask about the condition of Rydberg. He is heartened by the news that his friend is due back at work the next day. News of another murder linked to the current investigation jolts Wallander back into action. The drug dealer that Wallander was forced to release without charge is found shot in the back of the head, just like the two elderly sisters. Rydberg returns to work anxious to talk about the case rather than his illness.

Wallander struggles to make the connection between the series of deaths that have hit the province of Skåne but he is also preoccupied about his first Christmas since the divorce. He is lonely and unwilling to do anything about it but Linda saves the day by arranging his trip to Löderup to spend a happy holiday with his father. Wallander sees Linda use her good relationship with her grandfather to ensure the evening goes well. Sometimes Linda and his father get on so well that he feels as if he is on the outside but it doesn't bother him. Loneliness is quite heavily established as a major problem for Wallander throughout all the stories in *The Pyramid*.

As he struggles to move the investigation on he takes time out to go and visit his father again. He thinks that he again needs to experience the smell of oil paints that always reminds him of being a child. The mood of disenchantment among many of his colleague appears to be catching. While they plot alternative careers and escape routes, Wallander knows deep down that he must plough on with his chosen career. He is less sure about his 'increasingly anaemic' relationship with nurse Emma. He knows he is simply using her for sex and he is not proud of that knowledge. Wallander even envies his father his ambitious dreams that cause him to solo climb one of the pyramids and thus land his caring son with a massive bill.

Wallander tries to get his mind back onto the investigation. He is shocked by the rising tide of drugs that has made his job so much more difficult. After New Year, Wallander has a cold when Emma comes round and he is packed off to bed alone for once. He tries to find solace in his favourite book, *The Mysterious Island* by Jules Verne, but he is unable to concentrate fully. He knows that he is close to grasping the essential clue he needs to link and solve the murders and he gets it when he is at his father's house. Memories of the lights around the pyramids in Egypt suddenly start him thinking about the possibility of lights on the ground that might have guided in a late-night flight that is up to no good. Instantly, he is electrified with excitement as the likely possessor of lights is suddenly their number one suspect.

Wallander lives so much for his job that when he considers he and his team are on the right track it lifts his spirits so comprehensively that he even permits himself a rare light-hearted joke. An attractive young woman he is interviewing in a nightclub considers he is appraising her as a sex object and demands to know: 'Why aren't you looking me in the eye?' Wallander is not at all put off by the complaint and responds: 'That is probably because your skirt is so very short.' She bursts into laughter and the ice between them is broken. She recalls the recent theft of lights from the disco and Wallander is one step closer to nailing the villain.

As the net tightens around the killer Wallander again ignores one of the most basic rules of police work and puts himself in great danger without organising sufficient back-up. Fortune favours the brave and it certainly follows Wallander as he wins out in a dramatic shoot-out even though, as he himself admits, he is a terrible shot.

The Pyramid was published in Sweden in 1999 and translated into English and published in Britain in 2008.

Joan Smith in the *Sunday Times* wrote enthusiastically: 'Anyone who has ever wondered why Inspector Wallander is quite so hangdog will find the answer in *The Pyramid* by Henning Mankell. The idea behind this collection of Wallander stories is brilliant but simple: it consists of Wallander's earliest cases, beginning with a period in his life when he was still in uniform. The stories start with the apparent suicide of an elderly man and end with the brutal murders of two shopkeepers in Ystad, a case Wallander cracks after an unexpected dash to Egypt to get his cantankerous father out of trouble. As well as filling in gaps in Wallander's biography, the book reveals Mankell's sense that something has gone wrong in Sweden's model social democracy and identifies some of the causes of the malaise.'

CHAPTER FOUR:

FACELESS KILLERS

E urope is in turmoil as *Faceless Killers* opens. It is
January 1990, two months after the fall of the Berlin
Wall, and it is a time of enormous change as people
whose lives were once restricted to the grey old Soviet
bloc now find they are free to explore the colourful world
of the West. But as Wallander is introduced in the first
full-length novel, he hardly seems excited about the
tearing down of old borders. He is fast asleep at home in
the sleepy Swedish seaside town of Ystad, having stayed
up until the early hours of the morning listening to Maria
Callas sing her *Traviata* on his stereo system. He is also
alone, as his wife has left him some three months earlier,
but he is dreaming about making fierce and passionate
love to an unnamed black woman.

So in Mankell's very first paragraph about his now
internationally famous detective we learn that our new
hero is cultured, lonely and interested in sex, even when

he's dead to the world. But we are also soon to discover that he is perhaps not one of those most fervently gripped by the uplifting enthusiasm of the new decade. The popular joy at unprecedented levels of freedom being experienced by people from many different races does not overwhelm Wallander.

But before we have too much chance to form an opinion on the personality of our policeman, he is plunged into the grim task of solving a gruesome killing. Wallander is woken by a call from Ystad police station with the news that a murder has been committed in a remote farm in Lunnarp, some 20 kilometres to the north-east.

Wallander assures himself the call is genuine, slurps a cup of lukewarm coffee from a Thermos, and drives off to investigate. As he muses on the short drive, we find out that he is still deeply troubled by his wife's departure and also haunted by the time he was almost killed when he was a young policeman of 23, arresting a drunk who stabbed him with a butcher's knife.

The readers already know from a shocking first chapter that an elderly couple have been brutally attacked in their home. A neighbour is horrified to find farmer Johannes lying dead and his wife, Maria, tied to a chair and gravely injured. Even the experienced detective is shocked by what greets him at the murder scene. He finds the old couple's bedroom covered in blood. Johannes' face has been savagely mutilated. It appears, to Wallander's horror, that someone has attempted to cut off his nose. Fighting off his nausea, Wallander shouts for an ambulance and goes to do what he can to help Maria, who is cruelly trussed up with a noose around her neck and desperately close to death.

Maria is rushed to hospital and as the clearly determined detective heads back to the police station pondering over the grisly details of the horrific attack on defenceless old people, he suddenly receives a rare telephone call from his daughter, Linda. We learn that she is 19 and somewhat estranged from Wallander. When she calls, they have lost touch so completely that he does not know if it is from some unheard of place on the other side of the world, but it is from his near his home that she is ringing. She has called at his home on Mariagatan in central Ystad to visit. But now she is leaving without seeing him. Wallander is heartened by her attempt to make proper contact but it inclines him to muse on the troubled life of his only child. Linda tried to commit suicide when she was 15. The detective recalls how nothing more than an unexplained and sudden feeling of unease had led him to go into the bathroom, where he found his daughter had cut her wrists with a razor. His swift action to stem the bleeding saved her life. But all these years later he still has not the remotest idea of what led to the attempt to kill herself.

Another telephone call introduces another important character in Wallander's life: his difficult father. He is never given a first name in the books but the BBC films have christened him Povel. There's a hint of the dark humour that is an essential ingredient in the world of Wallander when we find out that his demanding father has been ringing the police station so often that his son has asked for the calls not to be put through. That prompts his father to take on several different fake identities in order to reach his son. Wary of this charade getting completely out of hand, Wallander reluctantly agrees to visit his father. Clearly, the two men have a complex and difficult relationship. Wallander Snr is an artist who paints the same scene over and over again, a landscape sometimes with a grouse in it, and sometimes without. He is deeply disappointed and, at times, angered by his son's decision to become a policeman but Kurt has not the remotest idea why. He asks his sister Kristina, who has a beauty salon in Stockholm, what their father wanted him to do in life rather than join the police but she has no clue. And his strong-willed father flatly refuses to discuss the matter any further.

Wallander is further troubled when he later visits to find his elderly dad living in a squalid state, but suggestions that Wallander Snr might be more comfortable, not to mention clean, in a retirement home are met with a furious response. The old man is outraged at the very idea he could be packed off to some kind of old people's home. He says he is fine with his housekeeper and is planning a trip to Italy where he is to have an exhibition. The outburst seems to stun Wallander, and the problems become more serious when the old man is found wandering around in his pyjamas with a packed suitcase. Wallander concludes, somewhat unemotionally, that his father is 'senile' and must be put into a home. But he rushes to find his father marching through a field. There is an angry confrontation and the suitcase bursts open to reveal dirty underwear and tubes of paint and brushes. Wallander realises that in his sadly deluded state his father was heading off to Italy. He drives his father straight to the emergency entrance of the hospital where an understanding doctor immediately admits him for the night for observation.

Music clearly plays an important role in the life of Kurt Wallander. As he attempts to forget his family worries and concentrate on the case, he consoles himself with the sound through the headphones of his Walkman of the late Swedish tenor Jussi Björling, singing songs from *Rigoletto* recorded in the 1930s. But even music he loves cannot prevent a shocking level of self-loathing. Wallander is horrified by his appearance in the mirror in the toilets at the police station. He looks bloated and overweight and he realises to his considerable horror that in the three months since his wife left him, he has put on seven kilos thanks to a diet of pizza, hamburgers and takeaways. He even says out loud to himself: 'You flabby piece of shit. Do you really want to look like a pitiful old man?' He vows inwardly to eat more healthily as he muses glumly that it is the fate of a policeman to be divorced. And his new eating regime ends, almost as soon as it begins, with a hamburger special that he eats so fast it sends him rushing to the toilet. Mankell spares few pieces of information about his flawed hero as we are told Wallander notices, as he is sitting on the toilet, that he ought to change his underwear.

If there is a single quality that shines through the pages from the very start of the literary life of Kurt Wallander then perhaps it is dedication. This policeman lives to solve crimes that come his way. That is what drives him on and that is why, after a busy day, he decides to take a long shift sitting by the badly injured victim in the hope she will say something that will lead the police to her attacker. But Maria dies while Wallander's colleague Rydberg is sitting with her. The only coherent thing she says before she passes away in her hospital bed is what could be the word 'Foreign', which is repeated several times. Wallander realises Maria could have been trying to tell them that her attackers were foreign and he also realises how much racial tension that information could inflame. There is a large refugee camp some 20 kilometres from the murder scene and feelings against asylum seekers are already running high among some Swedish people.

Of course, this is the broader subject that Henning Mankell set out to write about. He created Kurt Wallander to lead his readers into a story that is about much more than just another savage murder. Mankell had been horrified by a growing feeling of xenophobia in Sweden when he returned to his homeland from a spell in Africa. His country had long been a safe haven for people of all races. The opportunity for people from all over the world to integrate safely and happily into society was indeed an enviable one. Seeing Sweden through fresh eyes after his time away, Mankell detected a fundamental change in Swedish attitudes to immigrants that he wanted to explore and expose in print. But he did not want to write a didactic documentary-style work spelling out his fears. He knew that he could say what he wanted to say much more effectively if it was delivered within a novel about a crime. To tell the story he required a detective and he chose a man who was his age and with many of his own attitudes. 'But there are also many, many differences between myself and Kurt Wallander,' he said. Mankell knew that if he gave Wallander his own left-of-centre political views the novel would not work so well. He tried to make his new hero a sort of 'Everyman' figure with no fixed political agenda, apart from a firm belief in the importance of the rule of law. Mankell believed that way he would be perceived as a fair man with whom the readers would be able to comfortably identify.

When we first meet Wallander, we soon realise he is still reeling from the abrupt departure of his wife, Mona. Within a single October weekend she told her husband she wanted a divorce and moved out. She had already found herself a flat in Malmö, which she had rented in advance. Wallander had been both ashamed and angry at the sudden breakdown of his marriage and reacted very badly; he lost his temper and slapped his wife across the face. Regrets soon followed and he was overcome with grief at the end of his marriage. He appealed to Mona to try again and begged her to stay but she insisted she'd had enough of being married to a policeman who was married to his job.

Wallander visits an old friend called Sten Widen, supposedly to ask his advice as an expert horseman on the horse in the stables of the murdered couple. The knot on the rope with which the horse was tied up was unusual and Wallander thought it could be a key to identifying one of the attackers. The introduction of the hard-drinking

Widen is also a chance for Mankell to give his readers a few more details of his hero's past life and current state. Wallander and Widen have not seen each other for more than ten years but, in their twenties, they had been good friends who shared an outlandish ambition – to make a fortune out of an improbably upmarket area of showbusiness. Widen, who had a fine voice, was going to become a professional opera singer and Wallander was to be the skilful impresario who made him famous and successful. That unlikely youthful dream has long since faded but Wallander harbours hopes that there might still be a bond of friendship between them. Later he takes Widen to the scene of the crime to see if his expert knowledge of horses can yield any useful information. But the attempt is unsuccessful and the detective realises that his old pal does not want to rekindle anything.

Gradually the reader's picture of Wallander is being more fully drawn and coloured in. He is definitely a diligent and hard-working detective but he is often hopelessly unpractical. He is called back to the police station to hear of a new development but runs out of petrol on the way, and then finds he has no money or cards with him to buy some and has to borrow cash.

Maria's brother arrives at the police station insisting the murder must have been committed to rob Johannes, who was secretly very wealthy and unfaithful to Maria. It transpires that Johannes drew a large sum in cash from an account at the Union Bank in Ystad shortly before he was murdered. But just as it looks as if the investigation is getting somewhere, the news gets out that the police believe foreigners could be responsible. This is exactly what Wallander was concerned about and he is furious that someone within the police station must be leaking information to journalists. And while the threat of violence against any unfortunate foreigner looms large in police fears, Wallander gets another surprise when a woman called Anette Brolin takes over as prosecutor, his administrative superior. Wallander is happily surprised to find that she is young and very attractive. In his lonely and unhappy state he instantly starts thinking about asking her out, even though he knows perfectly well that she is married.

Wallander reveals early signs of his fortunate knack for being in the right place at the right time and he is just driving past the refugee camp when huts start bursting into flames. The place has been attacked by arsonists and Wallander bravely risks his life to try to drag people to safety. He is slightly injured and taken to hospital, managing to get himself photographed and hailed as a hero in the process. Mona sees the picture in the newspaper and telephones to see if he is all right. He immediately asks her to come back to him but she refuses, although she does agree to meet him for dinner.

Wallander insists he has recovered by the next day when he offers to take the appealing Anette out for lunch. The meal goes well and Wallander suggests dinner in a few days time. Anette accepts the offer. Mankell reveals to the readers that Wallander has fallen hopelessly in love with Anette, which is pretty poor timing as he has arranged to meet Mona in a supposed reconciliation attempt later that very night. But that is an encounter that goes very badly. Wallander is late after fortifying himself with whisky and being upset by a chance glimpse of Linda with a black boyfriend. He begs Mona to come back to him but she flatly refuses.

Wallander is devastated but a dreadful night gets worse when he is stopped, driving when unarguably drunk, by a police patrol car. He suddenly realises his career could be over as well as his marriage. It is a traumatic moment for Wallander. He knows he has allowed his disastrous private life to affect the job, which means everything to him. He has been a policeman for 20 years and now he is convinced it is finished. But the two coppers break the rules. One orders him into the back of the patrol car and the other drives his car home. Wallander gets a free ride home as well and he knows the two young officers have risked their own jobs to save his. He is ashamed and embarrassed and very grateful. It is a significant moment that forces Wallander to begin to look at the way he is living his life, although there is no instant move to restrict his drinking.

Wallander is in many ways uncomfortable with the changing times. He even struggles to set the alarm function on his watch. And when it comes to considering the future of his father, he has to discuss the situation with a social worker and we discover another hang-up. His long years of experience as a policeman have given him a serious aversion. Wallander profoundly distrusts social workers, whom he believes are too often misguided and forgiving when they should be prepared to take a harder line on more difficult cases. Previously he has railed against what he sees as some of Sweden's liberal welfare authorities who have failed to tackle young criminals and their illegal behaviour. There are many references to Wallander's affection for what he sees as the gentler days of years gone by. In a rush in his car as the murder investigation intensifies, he thinks he should have taken a squad car but then resolves that nowadays drivers are not so worried about getting out of anyone's way, even a policeman on urgent business. Wallander has a nostalgia for the past that is perhaps not uncommon in world-weary citizens of 40 but he does seem at times to be getting old before his years.

Above all, Wallander is seen to be human. He is no superman of detection. More than once he makes mistakes and late in the book, as the net of suspicion tightens around a retired policeman whose car is linked to the savage murder of a Somali refugee, Wallander realises as he leaves an interrogation that he has forgotten to ask two vital questions.

Rydberg is perhaps the closest thing Wallander has to a friend. The older officer is painfully thorough and not without a dry humour. As the police interest in a particular stolen Citroën grows, Rydberg says that there is a dermatologist from Lund, a nearby town, who is an expert on that make of car. Wallander is surprised and questions the source of this unlikely expertise. Rydberg responds dryly: 'There are hookers who collect stamps. Why shouldn't a dermatologist be into Citroëns?' It is the sort of remark that Wallander might appreciate. When he is going on a very chilly, all-night stake-out of the home of a suspect, he first goes for a meal and then drinks several cups of strong coffee. Then he buys a copy of *The Watch Tower* on the grounds that it would be 'sufficiently dull' to last him all night.

Like many maverick detectives Wallander breaks all the rules. When his suspect makes a late-night trip he follows him alone and falls and injures himself but only makes a joke of it afterwards. But one of the great things about Wallander is that he is forever unpredictable. In the middle of the tense arrangements to arrest dangerous subjects, he tells the alluring Anette that he would like to take her out for dinner.

When it comes to action Wallander is prone to making mistakes. He leads a team to arrest a man he believes could be a murderer and four armed officers somehow allow the man to escape. Wallander goes in hot pursuit and there is always a delicious hint of black humour in even the most serious situations. The suspected killer forces a driver from his car to make his getaway. Wallander, bleeding from a head wound and still struggling with the safety catch on his pistol, does the same, only he finds himself at the wheel of a large horsebox. The driver is out of the vehicle buying condoms from a machine. As soon as he sees Wallander he drops the condoms and runs for his life. The killer crashes into a concrete pillar and is himself killed. Wallander's horsebox slides into a ditch and topples over. Two horses are miraculously unhurt and freed in the incident to gallop away. It is only fractionally removed from something out of the *Keystone Cops* but somehow Mankell makes it remain breathtakingly believable at all times.

The reader is drawn in to sympathise with the deeply vulnerable Wallander and the way his chaotic private life keeps getting awkwardly entangled with his job. He forgets completely that he is supposed to be meeting his sister at the airport. She is flying over to see their father. Rydberg realises Wallander's mistake and arranges for a policeman to meet the flight. Later Wallander and his sister confront the squalor his father has been living in and decide they must hire a housekeeper, as the only man refuses to go into a retirement home. But Wallander ends this rare evening of family intimacy by asking Anette out for a drink. She agrees and they share a drink in her flat. With stunning social ineptness, Wallander contrives an argument about a case where the prosecutor refused permission to detain a man Wallander was convinced was guilty. He is provoked into revealing some of his heartfelt views on the breakdown of Swedish society. He raves against how law and order is being steadily eroded in his country and that no one cares about the increase in crime. He admits he can understand why people take the law into their own hands and says: 'The insecurity in this country is enormous.'

In perhaps the most moving scene in the whole remarkable book Wallander comes close to haranguing a woman he really wants to sleep with. He rants against the lack of a coherent policy on immigration that produces violence while Anette speaks up for the rule of law. It has been a year since he has made love to a woman and, although the mood between them has cooled following their argument, he lurches at her and makes a clumsy pass. The reaction is hardly one he wants or expects; Anette lashes out and slaps him across the face, her wedding ring cutting his cheek. She is furious. Wallander struggles to pull himself together and apologises. Anette says they will just forget it happened and shows him the door. It's a real low point for Wallander. He feels wretched and vows to stop drinking as he lurches sadly home. Next day he sends flowers and an apology to Anette. Later, as the investigation stalls for several weeks, Wallander and Anette go for long walks and even spend a night together in Copenhagen after going to the opera. Wallander is smitten and tells Anette he loves her but she does not feel the same way. It was just a night.

Mankell incorporates a good deal of information in the novel about the contemporary growth of neo-Nazi support. The men behind the savage shooting of the Somali refugee were found to be members of a racist underground network with political views close to that of the Ku-Klux-Klan in America. The uncomfortable background is carefully researched and such organisations were becoming more popular at the end of the 1980s and start of the 1990s when the book was written. Both Mankell and Wallander are most certainly from another, older world. But clearly they had very different views. The detective is not even sure of his own feelings with regard to Linda's black boyfriend, who turns out to be a Kenyan medical student. While Mona is pleased that she is happy in a relationship, Wallander is uncertain and guarded. But he is delighted when Linda at last gets in touch out of the blue and comes to visit. Father and daughter get on surprisingly well together and they visit Wallander's father, who delights them both by telling funny stories about Kurt as a boy.

But, almost as if the feel-good atmosphere cannot be allowed to dominate, Wallander receives some equally surprising bad news. Rydberg has been for tests and says that he has been diagnosed with prostrate cancer. He must have radiation treatment and chemotherapy and the prognosis is not especially good. He is blunt and abrupt and clearly does not want sympathy. Wallander is instantly robbed of his most perceptive colleague and his best friend, and gloom descends once more. The police might have solved the reprisal racist murder but they seem as far as ever from finding out who viciously killed Johannes and Maria.

Then Wallander has the sort of moment of inspiration that either entrances or irritates the reader. Personally, I am firmly in the former camp so what happens seems perfectly credible, but I know other readers and firm Wallander fans who felt slightly short-changed. What happens is that Wallander goes to the bank and stands in line behind a man who makes a very large cash withdrawal. While the man counts up the cash, Wallander absent-mindedly reads the name on the man's driving licence that he had put on the counter. It is not until Wallander walks out of the bank and onto the street that the idea hits him. Could Johannes have been spotted drawing out his 27,000 kronor in just the same way and then been targeted for robbery?

The clerk who paid out the money to Johannes is on

holiday but Wallander tracks her down to a beach, where she is engaged in a game of backgammon with friends and is wearing a miniscule bathing suit. She has an astonishingly good memory and recalls that Johannes was followed into the bank by two men who looked like foreigners. At last Wallander has a lead and the grim investigation suddenly picks up pace. The bank clerk is remarkably observant but six months have passed and all Wallander has, apart from her memory, is a scrawled signature on the foreigners' receipt. The bank clerk pores over photographs from the police files but then later she sees the two men again. They come into the bank and the clerk rings Wallander. By the time he gets there the two men have gone but she has had the presence of mind to activate the security cameras so now at last the police can see who they are searching for.

There are lots of blind alleys for Wallander to explore before he gets his men. During the hunt he finds time to visit Rydberg who is gloomy about his life expectancy. They talk and Wallander asks his friend if he has ever regretted becoming a policeman. Rydberg says: 'Never. Not once.' Eventually the two murderers are cornered at a market. After a chase and a violent struggle the killers are captured and later blame each other for the brutality of their acts. They came from Czechoslovakia and had previously gone into banks to seek out people withdrawing large amounts to later rob them.

As the intriguing murder mystery is finally solved, so facets of Wallander's chaotic private life become a little more ordered. He takes Anette Brolin to meet his father and asks her if she would consider getting a divorce so they could be together. She says no, but does not seem too upset to be asked. As the books ends he is spending a lot of time quietly drinking with Rydberg, who they both know is living on borrowed time.

This remarkable book was first published in Sweden in 1991. It received many favourable reviews and spearheaded the rise of Kurt Wallander. In Scandinavia and in Germany it became a best-seller and Mankell knew that he had a hit on his hands. But at the time it hardly registered in Britain and America. Later, in March 1997, Tom Nolan in the *Wall Street Journal* noted it as well worth reading and said: 'Kurt Wallander, the police detective in this European best-seller, exudes a Scandinavian gloominess to match his provincial corner's stark landscape and bleak weather. Creeping up on 43, the whiskey-drinking, opera-loving Wallander has lots to be depressed about: a failed marriage, a once-suicidal daughter he rarely sees and a father who may be going senile. Moreover, his country is undergoing disquieting change: Sweden is flooded with refugees seeking asylum; drug traffic has spread to the rural towns; and crime is taking a violent turn. Maybe the times require a new sort of policeman, Wallander muses: 'Cops who don't suffer from my uncertainty and anguish.' Provoking Wallander's angst are the brutal murders of an elderly farm couple. When word is broadcast that 'foreigners' are suspected, a random refugee is shotgunned in 'retribution' – and Wallander and crew must hunt for those killers, too.

Wallander has no fancy forensic tools. He catches crooks the old-fashioned way: through plodding routine, lucky leads and sudden inspiration. This type of socially conscious police procedural, in the hands of a gifted writer, can make for an especially satisfying crime novel, as demonstrated by such past masters as Georges Simenon, Nicholas Freeling and Sweden's own Maj Sjöwall and Per Wahlöö. With *Faceless Killers*, Henning Mankell seems to join those worthy ranks.'

On screen the BBC version ran in January 2010 and any Wallander fans hoping to see a faithful reproduction of the novel would probably have been sadly disappointed. It is simply not possible to convey the full events of one of Mankell's densely plotted and intricate *Wallander* adventures in 90 minutes. There was no Rydberg and his tragic news, no Anette and her dangerous liaison with our hero, and lots of the extraordinary happenings in Mankell's debut *Wallander* novel were missing from the screenplay. But the BBC version of *Faceless Killers* was, all the same, absolutely compelling from start to finish. Kenneth Branagh was masterful certainly but the excellent supporting cast were much more to the fore and the essential elements of the story were there for all to see.

CHAPTER FIVE:

THE DOGS OF RIGA

Kurt Wallander is reeling from a deep sense of personal loss as his second adventure begins. His closest friend Rydberg has died from the cancer that he developed towards the close of *Faceless Killers* and Wallander is deeply upset. Rydberg was his mentor in the police force and his advisor, as well as his closest and only real friend and he misses him very badly.

Wallander had known about the illness for a year and had visited Rydberg very often during that time. Rydberg knew all along that he was dying and faced his fate bravely while Wallander worried about how he would cope without his friend's judgement and wise counsel. When *The Dogs of Riga* opens, Rydberg has been dead less than a month and Wallander is feeling the pain and the loss very deeply. Fortunately for him at the time he has no difficult or desperately demanding cases, until a rubber life raft containing a pair of corpses is washed up on the beach.

The bodies are of two men, lying with their arms wrapped around each other. They are wearing suits and it appears from the first examinations that they have both been brutally tortured and then shot. Wallander looks grimly at the scene before the ambulance men are told to take the bodies away and, inevitably, wonders to himself what Rydberg would make of it all. Suddenly he misses the hunches and insights of his late friend even more, but Wallander is determined to discover how the two men met their end. He studies weather history and the movement of the tides to try to find out where the men came from. Meanwhile, an examination of the dead men's teeth concludes that they may well be from Russia.

Wallander is bewildered and just as he is feeling at his most confused about the case, his investigation is rudely interrupted by more personal problems. He wakes up at two o'clock in the morning with terrible chest pains and is convinced that he is about to die. He lies in the dark fretting about the complete mess he has made of his personal life. His normal mood is some way removed from a ray of sunshine but he is really down and feeling desperately sorry for himself at this point. Still in agony, he slowly gets out of bed and puts some clothes on. He goes down to the car and drives, still wracked with pain, to the Ystad hospital emergency area. There he is swiftly taken into a treatment room for tests. He is put on an ECG machine, has his pulse felt and his blood pressure taken. He explains that he doesn't smoke, has never had chest pains before and has no family history of heart problems. He also ignores the truth and says his alcohol consumption is normal!

His conversation with an understanding doctor calms his fears a little. The medic rules that he does not believe Wallander has had a heart attack but that he could be experiencing a wake-up call that he would do well to listen to. His overworked and overtired body is very probably sounding some sort of alarm. Wallander admits sadly that he has no one he can really talk to about such personal matters. The doctor shakes his head and replies gravely that everyone needs someone he or she can confide in and Wallander feels the personal agony of his isolation very acutely. He reveals the depths of his angst and says he worries every day what his life of rushed unhealthy meals, overwork and criminally unsocial hours is doing to him. It is a significant moment of introspection. He knows that what really troubles him is not his health but the difficult relationships he has with his father and daughter and the pain he still feels over his wife, Mona, walking out on him. In the hospital he feels completely desolate and he vows to himself to get his life sorted out once and for all.

Unfortunately, Wallander returns to work to a double dose of bad news. The case of the two corpses in the life raft seems to have hit a frustrating dead-end. And news comes through that one of the vicious murderers who killed the two old people at Lunnarp in *Faceless Killers* has somehow escaped from prison. Chief of Police Bjork tells Wallander that the man tricked the prison authorities into letting him out for his mother's funeral. Bjork and Wallander know that the man's mother died many years before, as the most rudimentary checks the

prison should have made would have uncovered.
Wallander thinks back to the shockingly savage double
murder and rages that it is pointless for them to be
rounding up criminals if they are not even going to serve
their sentences. He wonders again how long he can keep
going. Wallander feels deeply disillusioned with his life in
the police and has even considered applying for a job as
head of security for a Swedish rubber company. He
reflects sadly that he feels he has become alarmingly 'old
fashioned', even though he is only 43 years old.

Wallander might not be as close to his father as he
would like but he does realise that the old man finds a
great sense of security from his ability to paint the same
melancholy sunset over and over again. So he happily
offers to take his father to Malmö for more paints,
brushes and canvases, and they plan to go for a meal
together afterwards. Wallander's father has refused to
tidy himself up for the trip in spite of heavy hints from
his son. Afterwards, when Wallander reminds his father
they need to find a restaurant, to his surprise his father
enthusiastically agrees though he comically insists the
head waiter finds them a good table when they go into in
a humble self-service cafeteria. The encounter has the
two men interacting a little at last, though Wallander
reacts badly to his father's bluntness. His father asks
awkward questions about how Linda is doing and
whether Wallander has found a new woman. When he
gets no satisfactory answer, his father asks if he is 'still
sulking' over Mona. Wallander listens to his father tell
him bluntly that he is getting odder and odder as he gets

older and he bitterly resents the judgement. The rift between the two men remains unbridged but at the same time Wallander begins to realise he is in danger of getting more and more like his father – that is to say, becoming pig-headed and incapable of seeing anything he doesn't want to see.

The investigation into the two corpses found in the drifting life raft is suddenly complicated when details of the case start appearing in the newspapers. Clearly there is a leak from within the Ystad police and stories about 'Soviet death patrols' hardly help. Wallander is puzzled by the involvement of the Swedish foreign ministry as he tries to track down exactly from where the two men could have drifted across the Baltic. The man from the ministry turns out to be a woman and lonely Wallander quickly asks her out for dinner, but is politely rebuffed. That does nothing for his growing sense of insecurity and he again considers leaving the police force.

To cheer himself up he turns to Maria Callas singing *La Traviata*, which seems to be his favourite piece of music. News comes from the police in Riga, the capital of Latvia, that there is a good chance the dead men came from their city. Major Liepa from the Latvian police arrives to assist with the investigation. Wallander imagines that, as the murders did not appear to have been committed in Swedish territory, this will be the end of any involvement by the Ystad police.

But it doesn't turn out like that at all. The Latvian policeman turns out to be a small guy with a badly hunched back who insists on chain smoking in all of the

'No Smoking' areas of the police station. Most of the Swedish police think he is out of order but typically Wallander reacts very differently and really warms to the sharp-witted and hard-working officer. And the story that Major Leipa tells of the two murder victims enthrals and fascinates Wallander. Evidently the two men were violent Russian criminals with powerful links to the Mafia and the secret police. They had been operating in Latvia for some time and had always had some influential protectors to keep them out of prison. Wallander becomes further intrigued by the case after the life raft itself is stolen from inside the police station. But then the case is transferred back to Riga and Wallander thinks it is all over for him. Major Liepa goes home and takes the bodies with him. Wallander has built up a good relationship with the little Latvian and has formed a great respect for his dogged powers of detection. But only a few days after the Major's return home, the shocking news comes from Latvia that he has been cold-bloodedly murdered. Without having any say in the matter, Wallander is flown to Riga to help with the Latvian investigation.

If Wallander feels insecure with life in his native Sweden, then he feels totally lost in the dark intrigue of Latvia, where the process of law, like everything else, appears to be dominated by the country's superpower neighbour, Russia. He is caught between two high-ranking police officers, Colonel Putnis and Colonel Murniers, who are in charge of finding the killer or killers of Major Liepa. Today the streets of Riga might echo to the drunken antics of stag and hen parties from Great Britain, Germany and other countries, but back in 1991 there is little sign of raucous or wild behaviour. Although the native Latvians are moving towards independence from Russia, there is still much influence and control from Moscow in these troubled times. Wallander is like a fish out of water in a country struggling to emerge from the yoke of communism. He knows that his every movement is being watched and feels uncomfortable and suspicious. Back in Sweden, Major Liepa had tried to explain how difficult it was to operate an independent police force when the Russian secret service had infiltrated so many high offices. Wallander is on his guard but he is still staggered when Major Leipa's widow makes contact with him at his hotel disguised as a chambermaid. She makes it clear that even in his official capacity there is danger everywhere and it is hard to tell who to trust. Wallander manages to elude his minders long enough to be smuggled out of his official hotel to talk to the only person he feels he can trust, Major Leipa's widow, Baiba.

They arrange a clandestine meeting at an organ recital in a church and as he anxiously waits for her to arrive, the music sooths him and reminds him of a childhood visit to church with his father. Back then the organ music had frightened him so much that he had burst into tears, but now he finds the music deeply comforting. He is reassured that the magic of Bach can cross all borders. The importance of music to detective Wallander is emphasised again as he sees Baiba in a nearby pew and they both wait for the end of the concert before they can meet. Wallander reflects that only a few weeks previously her husband had been sitting, alive and well, on his sofa in Sweden listening to Maria Callas sing *Turandot*. Now the Major is dead and he is in a church in Latvia with Leipa's widow listening to a Bach fugue. Wallander feels that his life has turned totally upside down in a very short time.

When he meets Baiba after the concert, she reveals that after years of undercover investigation her husband had discovered a massive conspiracy of evil involving very senior figures in the country. He had found out about a link between politicians, police and the criminal gangs. There was a secret government department set up to co-ordinate this criminal conspiracy. But Major Leipa's discoveries were to be his downfall. Baiba tells Wallander her husband was betrayed and murdered because of what he had found out. She believes one of the two colonels, who are his immediately superior officers, was responsible her husband's death. She fills Wallander in on the grim reality of life under Russian control. The Iron Curtain might have been pulled back in many stretches of Europe but in Latvia life still does not feel very free.

Wallander is outraged and determined to do what he can to help Baiba. But all of a sudden the colonels announce that they have found the man responsible for killing Major Liepa, and Wallander soon finds that his stay in Latvia is drawing to an early close. He realises that either Colonel Putnis or Colonel Murniers must be involved in the huge conspiracy and be responsible for the Major's death, but crucially he does not know which one of them. Alone and under constant observation, Wallander feels completely helpless. He is determined to get to the bottom of this injustice but he is also gripped by another emotion; he has fallen hopelessly in love with Baiba Liepa. All of Wallander's worries about his safety and security seem forgotten now he is gripped by this fierce and dangerous passion.

As his time in Latvia ticks away, Baiba pleads with him to return secretly and help. They realise that the Major must have hidden details of his inquiries somewhere and that somehow they must find them. Wallander agrees to come back with a false identity and a forged passport and try to solve the mystery. He flies home to Sweden and is relieved to no longer have the feeling he is being shadowed all the time. Yet while he is certainly pleased to be home, even as he returns to Sweden he questions everything about his nation's attitudes. The woman at immigration control ignores his friendly greeting and Wallander muses on the contrast between Sweden's bright and shiny exterior and the people's behaviour, which prevents them from talking to strangers. Wallander dislikes the view that anything new or unfamiliar must be viewed with great suspicion, as it could somehow possibly threaten the illusion of their perfect world.

The integrity of Mankell's Swedish policeman shines through almost every scene as he resolves to return in secret to Latvia to face what he knows will be real danger. The 'dogs' of Riga are the sinister security patrols who he knows will try to follow his every move and possibly even threaten his life, but he is also now motivated by love. He begins to believe he can bring Baiba Leipa back to Sweden and they can have a life together. He even tells his father about his new love and is urged to bring her back and marry her. Wallander's father is firm that his son needs to have more children. There is a rare moment of closeness between the two men and Wallander confides in his father that he is considering quitting the police for good very soon and taking a job as a security officer. But deep down Wallander remains troubled. He visits a restaurant in Ahus where there is a dance band and he finds himself whisking Ellen, a physiotherapist from Kristianstad, round the floor. She invites him to join her at her table but Wallander can't get Baiba's face out of his mind and he makes his excuses and leaves. That night, back in his flat in Ystad, he drinks himself into a stupor and turns his music up so loud the neighbours start thumping on the walls.

When the message finally comes from Latvia preparing the plans for his return, it is hidden in some junk mail. Ever inquisitive, Wallander can never resist reading everything that comes through his inbox, thanks to his compulsion to 'turn over every stone', so he makes the contact. He takes leave from work, using a 'skiing trip' to disguise his absence from the police station in Ystad, and he eventually enters Latvia by land through a remote southern forest. He is very determined to find Major Leipa's hidden 'testimony' that will bring the guilty men to justice. From the start it is not easy and many times Wallander questions his own conviction. With the highly unconvincing cover that he is a German businessman, trusted helpers see to it that he makes it cross-country without the authorities discovering his whereabouts. As he makes his dangerous and covert trip, Wallander remains desperate to see Baiba again but becomes increasingly convinced that he could well be out of his mind. At one point he is certain he is doing the stupidest thing he has ever done in his life and thinks that perhaps he has completely lost his sense of judgement and gone out of his mind. But he has gone much too far to turn back now so, with a heavy heart and frequently looking over his shoulder in terror, he carries on.

Over the border Wallander is met by some of Baiba's loyal friends, including a beautiful girl called Inese. She too believes that he will somehow find the vital details of Major Leipa's incriminating investigation and successfully complete the case that will help to clean up Latvia. It is a desperately tall order and it soon becomes much harder when the police attack and kill Inese and her helpers. Wallander has seen violence many times before but he is shocked rigid by the needless cruelty. He manages to escape but he is outraged by the carnage and in fear of his life. He is really up against it but shows enormous resourcefulness and great courage, especially when he manages to steal Major Leipa's diligently compiled evidence from deep inside police headquarters. It reveals a complex and cynical conspiracy to use highly organised international drug smugglers to enrich crooked policemen and politicians, while at the same time cleverly discrediting the Latvian national movement by making it appear that it is linked with the evil narcotics trade.

In the end the crooked Colonel is unmasked and killed in another savage shoot-out and Wallander and Baiba Leipa struggle to come to terms with the complexity of their feelings for each other. He spends the night with her in her tiny flat before returning to Sweden but, although passion is raging like never before within the loins of the stolid Swede, he is destined to be disappointed as they sleep separately. On the sofa, Wallander can hear her calm breathing from the bedroom as he remains sleepless despite his almost complete exhaustion. The honest surviving Colonel takes Wallander and Baiba to the graves of Inese and their brave friends and they both weep openly. It is a heart-rending experience for Wallander. He has never experienced anything quite like it. Wallander cries like a baby in total despair. He and Baiba do hug each other tightly before he is taken to the airport for his flight back to Sweden but there are no expressions of love or indications that there might be a future meeting between the two of them. Back in Ystad, Wallander turns down the offer of an interview for the job of security officer even though he is still by no means certain that spending the rest of his life as a police officer is what he wants to do. He writes a long and emotional letter to Baiba, spelling out all his feelings, and then tears it up. He does not know what he really wants to say to her.

So an enthralling second outing for Wallander ends

with readers surely feeling they know much more about the sad and so often dysfunctional Swede. It's a brilliant book which does much to educate readers about what life must have been like in nations such as Latvia that emerged often painfully from grim years under brutal Russian control. Henning Mankell adds a thoughtful afterword thanking two sources, one of them an unnamed detective in the Riga homicide squad for helping him to provide what felt like such an authentic backdrop to his thrilling story. It was only a few months after Mankell finished writing, in the spring of 1991, that the coup took place in Moscow that helped lead to independence for Baltic countries including Latvia, so that country is now changed for ever. *The Dogs of Riga* succeeds on many levels, not least as a disturbing slice of recent history.

But it also marked a huge chapter in the development of Wallander. Just about every facet of his life is challenged in this enthralling book, from his health to his sanity and from his devotion to the police to his future happiness. The reader, I think, comes away knowing much more about the lonely policeman from Ystad and also liking what they know. Certainly they finished this book wanting to know more and to read more, and happily Mankell was there to oblige us all.

The Dogs of Riga was first published in Sweden in 1992 but the English translation did not arrive until 2001. It was widely hailed as a triumph in this country. The *Observer* noted that: 'Henning Mankell is in the first division of crime writing.' And in the *Sunday Times*, Donna Leon commented thoughtfully: 'The ending, where the villain pops out of a doorway almost like a character in a pantomime, shows that this is an early book (the second in the *Wallander* series, in fact), but it is filled with the rich promise of the talent that is fully realised in Mankell's later books.'

CHAPTER SIX:
THE WHITE LIONESS

There is nothing quite like a good old-fashioned row with his father to really infuriate Wallander. He can deal with gun-toting killers without getting close to losing his temper but a bust-up with his father never fails to make him lose his cool. As *The White Lioness* begins, Wallander is still seething from another angry argument with his cantankerous dad. This time his father has shocked Wallander by suddenly announcing that he is going to get married. Wallander tells his father that it is ridiculous. He says bluntly that he is almost 80 years old and should certainly not be heading for any wedding bells.

But Wallander Snr is adamant and he mischievously challenges his son to guess the identity of the lucky lady. Kurt soon works out that the bride-to-be is his father's faithful cleaner, housekeeper and foot-washer, Gertrud, and he furiously points out that she is at least 30 years younger than he is. Kurt begins to lose his cool and tells his father he has never been able to live with another person, but the response from Povel, to use his BBC name, is that he has become much more easy-going and better tempered in his old age. Kurt is almost speechless with incredulity. But not quite; the two men argue angrily until Kurt's father hurls his coffee cup into the tulip bed and locks himself into the shed he uses to paint his pictures. Kurt storms off and drives home much too fast, only to find that his flat has been burgled and damaged, and his new stereo equipment and many of his beloved CDs and records stolen. When he arrives at work he is still incandescent with rage, which is hardly the best mood in which to meet a man who introduces Wallander to his next great adventure and challenge. Robert Åkerblom is a very anxious estate agent and he has come to the police station to report his wife missing.

We readers already know that Louise Åkerblom has been callously shot dead by a mysterious stranger without any apparent motive, apart from the fact that she had disturbed him at a house she was visiting in the course of her job. Privately, Wallander comes to the conclusion that it is possible that something unpleasant has happened to the religious mother-of-two, but he tries not to raise Robert Åkerblom's fears any further. After he has interviewed the anxious husband Wallander reflects on his feelings for Baiba Leipa, the only woman he is linked with romantically. Although he has not seen her for a year, he has not been able to forget her. And he admits to himself that he has been trying very hard.

Nostalgia is a frequently recurring theme in all

Wallander stories. The hero and, presumably, the writer, yearn for the simpler, gentler days of years gone by. As Wallander searches for the missing woman he is still haunted by the memory of the savage murder scene he encountered at the start of *Faceless Killers*. He shudders at the memory of finding the old farmer and his wife brutally beaten in their remote farmhouse. Then at least he had the wisdom and experience of his old colleague Rydberg to lean on in his most difficult moments. But as he fears finding the corpse of Louise Åkerblom in similarly distressing circumstances, he repeatedly asks himself what is happening in Sweden. What has happened to the old style villains and crooks who might have been dishonest in the extreme but were rarely mindlessly cruel? The sweeping upsurge in savage and pointless violence that he has seen overwhelm his country in his years as a policeman deeply troubles him.

And breaking bad news is something that Wallander never gets used to. After years of experience of delivering the very information that he knows will shatter the lives of the people he is speaking to, he never finds it any easier. After Louise Åkerblom is found at the bottom of a well with a bullet hole in her forehead, he goes with a heavy heart to give the grim information to her husband. The couple have two young daughters who, mercifully, are not at home but it is still a thankless task. Wallander takes the family's vicar with him. He tries to be as sympathetic as he can but he knows all the time that he must search for possible clues in the husband's reaction. Mankell brings the reader brilliantly back to earth after this uncomfortably emotional encounter as he has Wallander experiencing a mixture of unease and hunger as he leaves the house. He stops for a hamburger to deal with at least one of his needs.

The plot certainly thickens when a black finger is found near the murder site and a remote farmhouse is blown up. The police find themselves appealing for help from the public, which prompts a rare moment of light-heartedness from Wallander. Some of the contributions are so bizarre that he tells his colleague, Svedberg, that he is considering writing a book called *People Who Want To Help The Police*. He says he knows it would make him rich because, apart from the small number of useful pieces of information, he could include details of all the weird and half-baked tips that are inevitably produced by any police request for information.

Wallander always takes his work home with him and frequently it appears to him after he has gone to sleep in dream form. Clearly the discovery of the finger of a black man has etched its way into his subconscious as he dreams that one of his hands has gone black. His trusted old colleague Rydberg, who has been dead for almost two years, comes into the dream and questions why only one of the hands is black. Wallander wakes up wondering why he then insisted that something important would happen later that day. As it turns out, the only important thing that occurs is the elimination of a possible suspect. Wallander is left feeling depressed and frustrated at his inability to tie up so many loose ends and find Louise Åkerblom's killer. He feels haunted by the sinister solitary black finger and begins to feel that it is pointing accusingly at himself. At one point he drives to a car park by beautiful Krageholm Lake, walks to the water's edge, sits on a damp rock and reflects that he is just as troubled by his own unhappy personal life as he is by the apparently insoluble case. Somehow he knows he is on the fringe of the sort of ruthlessly cruel and murderous activity that he has never experienced before. This is a level of violence that he knows he will never be able to comprehend or deal with. Ordinary robbers and murderers with a simple motive are people he is confident he can tackle but he muses that it will be for the next generation of policemen to deal with the new kind of crimes.

This investigation does appear to get even deeper under Wallander's skin than the previous two cases. When a young policeman called Engman excitedly admits that this is the first time he has hunted a murderer, Wallander sharply warns him never to forget that in Sweden a man is innocent until proven guilty. As soon as he has made the remark, he regrets its harsh tone and resolves to make up for it by saying something kind – but then realises he can't think of anything!

Wallander is correct when he assumes he is on the fringe of criminal operations of which he can have no concept. Mankell then opens the door to the reader on a plot of monstrous evil being hatched far away in South Africa. In April 1992, as the country so long riven by the strife and injustice of apartheid struggles to move on from its violent past, the future depends on the will of two men, President de Klerk and the iconic figure of freedom fighter Nelson Mandela. History has shown what these two men achieved but Mankell chooses that moment in history to invent a hideous assassination plot that would have plunged South Africa into more bloodshed. Evil agents within the government who are determined to cling onto white supremacy at all costs conspire to murder Mandela. A black hitman called Mabasha is sent to faraway Sweden to be trained for his sickening task by Anatoli Konovalenko, a former KGB officer. It is this deadly duo that luckless Louise Åkerblom stumbles into when she searches for a remote house that is to be put on sale. Neither men are strangers to doling out death but when Konovalenko is disturbed by this unwanted visitor, he does not hesitate to shoot her dead. Mabasha is sickened by this needless murder and the cruel act sparks a rift between the two men that propels the narrative to scintillating levels of excitement. Mabasha tells Konovalenko he is going to kill him but the two men fight and Mabasha has a finger cut off before he rushes off, leaving Konovalenko for dead. However, the ruthless Russian is only unconscious and he sets out determined to find and execute Mabasha.

Konovalenko robs a bank to raise money to put a price on Mabasha's head in the Swedish underworld. As he flees the scene a police car appears and Konovalenko ruthlessly shoots dead a young policeman. Wallander is still bewildered as he struggles to establish how the crimes are linked but he is, more than ever, desperate to tackle the vile culprit of these chilling murders. He thinks to himself that he is 44 years old and already feeling worn out. In one particularly low moment he turns, not for the first time, to drink. He goes to a dance club and drinks whisky but the popular music makes him feel even more unhappy, and he abandons the idea of trying to pick up a woman as he rushes outside to be violently sick. Back home he makes a drunken telephone call to Baiba Leipa in Riga and tells her how much he loves her. But she is frightened by the late night phone call and the conversation goes badly. He apologises and consoles himself with a half bottle of vodka. Next day he is full of regrets and sits watching television and feeling sorry for himself.

Wallander knows that, generally, being part of the team is essential for successful police work but he somehow takes this case so personally that he begins investigating alone. He goes to a disco popular with Africans where he believes he might find a lead to the man with the missing finger and he finds himself hot on the trail of Konovalenko. He ploughs into action alone and alerts the wary Russian that he is the subject of a manhunt. All of a sudden and without knowing it, Wallander has gone from being the hunter to the hunted. Konovalenko is an expert and callous assassin and he is on Wallander's trail.

With desperately dangerous timing, Wallander chooses the moment to effect something of a reconciliation with his spirited daughter Linda. He finds she has grown into a more attractive and assertive woman and he is shocked to discover that she knows all about his affection for Baiba Leipa. Linda opens up about how difficult she found her childhood with parents who never really discussed the important things of life with her. Linda accuses her father of being interested only in things like tulip bulbs in the garden, new taps in the bathroom and, of course, his work. But although they cover difficult territory between them it is a warm encounter and Wallander teases her by asking her how she can walk in such high heels. Linda says you get used to them and asks if he would like to try. The gentle humour somehow bonds them and Wallander is delighted to be repairing their relationship.

But this rare outbreak of family harmony causes Wallander to take his eye off the ball in his murder hunt. He does not realise that he is becoming a target as both Mabasha and Konovalenko start to shadow the detective in order to find their enemy. Mabasha sneaks up on Wallander and lays him out with a single punch. When he comes round Wallander realises to his horror and embarrassment that he has been kidnapped. When Konovalenko attacks the African there is a chance to escape and Wallander manages to get away in the confusion. He rushes to make sure Linda is safe. He now realises his enemies know everything about him and that Linda is in great danger herself. The African tracks Wallander down to his home and then comes a curious twist. Against all rules of police procedure, Wallander decides that he can trust Mabasha and accepts that they can secretly help each other. Linda is astonished to find that his father is now trying to help Mabasha, the same man that hit him. Wallander is completely convinced of the truth of Mabasha's story that it was Konovalenko who killed Louise Åkerblom, and decides he must get the

African out of the country. That means providing him with a false passport.

This controversial decision reveals something of the depth of the humanity of Wallander. He knows Mabasha is a hitman who was training for another deadly mission in Sweden but he believes his regrets over the death of Mrs Åkerblom are sincere and thinks that he deserves another chance. This seems like putting himself out on an extremely slender limb, given that it involves breaking the law as well as all police rules. To be fair, the decision comes only after much soul-searching on the part of Wallander. He suffers pangs of conscience because he knows that in many ways what he is doing is questionable. But he believes it is the only way he can get the situation under control. Wallander makes Mabasha promise he will destroy the false passport the day he arrives back in Africa and the African solemnly agrees. It's a time of great turmoil in the life of Wallander. A KGB-trained killer is out there somewhere determined to end his life. He is still troubled as to whether he is doing the right thing over Mabasha. Then he gets the news that it is Louise Åkerblom's funeral. He decides to go, even though he hates funerals with a passion. We learn that some 11 years previously he broke down at his mother's funeral and was unable to read the planned address. Instead he rushed from the church in a terrible state.

But before Wallander can get Mabasha and his forged passport safely out of the country, Konovalenko and accomplices mount a terrifying night-time attack that costs the African his life and leaves our hero in grave danger. Wallander is traumatised to see the African shot right in front of his eyes. To save his own life Wallander has to shoot dead Konovalenko's sidekick, Rykoff, and then he sets off in an almost demented pursuit of the Russian. Svedberg and Martinsson are confronted by their senior officer looking crazed, with a pistol in one hand and a shotgun in the other. They conclude that Wallander is on the edge of a breakdown and that the stress of the case is clearly telling on him. Back at the police station they discuss Wallander's fragile mental condition with their boss, Bjork. They consider everything from drink to Alzheimer's and clearly have no clue at all as to what is really troubling him.

Mankell describes Wallander's thought processes with great delicacy and sensitivity. It seems the dedicated policeman becomes so set on catching Konovalenko that he forgets all concepts of correct police procedure. He becomes convinced that only he, acting alone, and through the most secret and unofficial channels, can apprehend the ruthless Russian, and almost nothing else matters. The intensity of the closing chapters of the book is quite extraordinary. Wallander is behaving very strangely, yet the reader can perfectly well understand, and indeed sympathise with, his motives. In his desperation Wallander turns not to his police colleagues for help, but to his old friend, the heavy-drinking horse-breeder Sten Widen. The baffled police put out an appeal for help from the public in finding Wallander, as well as locating Konovalenko. The police are forced to inform the public that Wallander might not be 'in full possession of his faculties'. Wallander decides that being a detective inspector who is temporarily out of his mind is just the excuse he needs to track down his prey alone. He knows that it will probably be impossible to arrest the Russian without loss of life and decides that is a sacrifice he will make.

But Konovalenko is cunning and resourceful, as well as monstrously evil. Wallander persuades Svedberg to put a guard on Linda and his father but Konovalenko tricks them and snatches Wallander's daughter. He cuts Linda's hair off and sends it to Wallander to prove she is his hostage. All of a sudden Wallander's worst nightmare has come true. His only daughter is in the hands of a homicidal maniac who is determined to kill him. It hits Wallander 'like an attack of vertigo'. He flies into a rage and rips the telephone from the wall after getting the call with the devastating news. Widen watches his friend's torment with growing horror but there is nothing he or anyone can do to ease Wallander's agony. He is distraught that the person he cares for most in the world has been kidnapped, simply because of her relationship to himself. Konovalenko knows that Linda is Wallander's weak spot. He knows the dogged policeman will come to try to free his daughter and he pledges to kill both of them when the time comes. Svedberg pleads with Wallander to allow them to help rescue Linda but the answer is a firm, 'No'. Wallander believes if the police get officially involved it will lead to Linda's death. He is convinced he alone can save Linda. This maverick attitude in this case is rooted not in machismo but, apparently, in realism. Wallander honestly believes that if the police find where Linda is being held and then surround the house, it will inevitably end in a massive shoot-out and her death. He is as measured and pragmatic as he can manage but later, when he receives the package containing Linda's hair and a necklace he once gave her, he breaks down in tears.

Faithful Svedberg understands his boss's orders to do nothing but refuses to obey them. He is convinced that Wallander needs help, now more than perhaps at any time in his life. Svedberg cleverly follows up a lead to the Russian's female assistant, Tania, and discovers the house where Konovalenko is holding Linda. But Wallander still insists on acting alone and prepares himself for an early morning meeting with the man who is holding his daughter hostage. However, Tania has a conscience and she has come to hate Konovalenko, the man who has brought so much death and cruelty into her life. She feels sorry for Linda, lying shackled and shaved in her 'cell'. Tania waits until the Russian has gone to sleep and then sneaks down to the cellar where Linda is being imprisoned and frees her. But as Linda bolts for freedom she makes a noise that wakes Konovalenko. He is furious that Linda has escaped and in his rage savagely murders Tania with stomach churning cruelty.

When Wallander finds the house and goes inside, Konovalenko has vanished but the viciously mutilated body of Tania remains. At first Wallander thinks it is his daughter who is lying in front of him. When he realises it is the luckless Tania he rushes outside to be violently sick. Svedberg spells out the sadistic fury that was inflicted on

Tania and says he shudders to think what the last hour of her life was like. Wallander returns to his father's house and is shocked to find that Linda is there, sleeping peacefully after her horrific ordeal. He stares at her hair, cropped short on one side of her head, and then lies down on the floor next to her bed and goes to sleep. Next day Linda cuts the other side of her hair and refuses all her father's entreaties to see a doctor.

Wallander phones Bjork and says he has had some sort of a breakdown and that he needs more time off to get over his ordeal. He lies to Bjork that he is staying in a small hotel in Copenhagen to recuperate. But instead he goes back to the house where Linda was held hostage to search for clues to where Konovalenko might have gone. He finds a faint pencil mark on a map and heads off for the marked area, where he tracks down the man he is determined to bring to justice. It seems like a long shot but it pays off and Wallander, now completely focussed on dealing with the man who threatened his daughter's life, finds the Russian's hideaway. The brave detective pulls his gun and confronts Konovalenko, who manages to flee the scene in a Mercedes. The men exchange shots but the car chase is short and very final. One of the rear tyres of Konovalenko's car is punctured by a bullet from Wallander and the Mercedes crashes into a huge concrete barrier next to a bridge. Wallander is so determined to wipe out the Russian that he smashes his car into the crashed Mercedes and then fires his gun at it, causing the car to burst into flames. Konovalenko's body is hurled halfway through the windscreen by the impact of the crash and then roasted by the fire. Wallander is instantly elated but the real impact of the horrendous sequence of experiences he has been through is soon to make its mark.

Wallander's mental state is desperately fragile as he struggles to get back to normal after this extraordinary adventure. As soon as he takes in the shock of Konovalenko's death, the feeling of overwhelming relief is very quickly replaced by a deep depression that completely devastates him. While the hunt for the evil assassin was going on there seemed to be some form of automatic pilot which sustained Kurt Wallander. It was almost as if he had not got time to be ill so his mind and body kept functioning well enough to take on Konovalenko. But as soon as he sees the Russian burned alive in front of him on the Öland Bridge, which goes from Kalmar in Sweden across the water to Färjestaden on the island of Öland, it is as if vital parts of his system begin to shut down. He tells Linda later that it was as if at that very moment a countdown to complete blankness began. He feels every reason for living has disappeared into a terrible misery which has mysteriously enveloped him.

Wallander simply stares into space and allows other police officers to take over and deal efficiently with the aftermath of the shocking crash. Later he is left sitting quietly on his own in the police station at Kalmar as the demand for information from a growing number of newspapers and radio and television stations is handled. The local police are careful not to trouble the bewildered looking detective from Ystad. Then there is a complete change in Wallander and a sudden burst of energy as he demands to be taken back to the house where Konovalenko had been hiding. His wish is instantly granted. The man in charge of the scene politely defers to Wallander when he marches around insisting that a search is mounted for Konovalenko's accomplice, who appears to have completely vanished. The man responsible for the house is found to be a neo-Nazi supporter and he receives a hard time from Wallander in full flow, determined to discover every single possible fact about the mysterious missing companion.

Wallander tries to assure Linda that he is fine and that they can go away for a few days holiday together. Bjork is angry that Wallander has lied to him about his whereabouts and gone off in search of Konovalenko alone. Wallander is outraged to have his behaviour challenged in such a way and angrily slams down the telephone. Bjork is astonished. Wallander has never done anything like that before. He believes that the outburst confirms his view that Wallander is still unbalanced and unfit for police duty. He warns Martinsson and Svedberg that they will have to keep a close watch on their respected but clearly unwell colleague. Once the search of the house is concluded Wallander flips out and drives off at high speed on a remote road through the forest. He is racing along, without his seat belt fastened, when a huge bull moose wanders into the road. Wallander just manages to brake in time. He knows he should feel elated to have escaped a crash and a serious injury or worse but instead he is left with a sickening feeling of unease. What he really wants, he thinks miserably to himself, is to walk off into the forest and never come back. His depression engulfs him all over again with even more power.

In spite of his precarious mental state, Wallander is desperate to get a message through to the authorities in South Africa. He knows it is vital to bring about the arrest of the assassin, trained by Konovalenko after the death of Mabasha, who has taken over the vile task of killing the country's saviour, Nelson Mandela. This brings new angst for Wallander as his initial missive fails to arrive due to an infantile administrative error. Only just in time does the vital message get through to save the life of the great statesman. The international element to this fascinating novel is expertly handled and provides a compelling backdrop to the adventure. But the reader's concern is repeatedly brought back to the fragile condition of Wallander, who broke all the rules of Swedish policing to take on alone the hideous threat posed by the most ruthless organised criminals. He clearly believed this unorthodox approach was the right course of action, in fact the only possible course of action in the circumstances, but it takes a terrible toll on him. His emotions at this time are very mixed and extremely confused but central to them at all times is a burning sense of regret at having killed a man. He knows perfectly well, of course, that when he shot Konovalenko's fat helper Rykoff there was no alternative, other than sacrificing his own life. But in doing so he has allowed the most evil villain he has ever encountered to escape.

Wallander is formally signed off sick as soon as the

operation is over. The doctor who treats him is confronted with a wide range of disturbing symptoms. Wallander is unable to pinpoint exactly what is wrong with him but he is suffering from such contrasting conditions as horrific nightmares and a serious inability to sleep. At times he bursts into uncontrollable sobbing. He also has crippling stomach pains and terrifying panic attacks. The doctor prescribes anti-depressants which he thinks might help counter Wallander's guilt. As well as the death of Rykoff, Wallander deeply regrets the killing of Mabasha, the would-be assassin he befriended, as well as the agonising, tortured death of Tania, who lost her life helping to save hostage Linda. Wallander is even traumatised by the spectacular death of Konovalenko, however much he tries to convince himself that it was richly deserved. Police colleagues like Svedberg and Martinsson begin to fear that their revered leader will never return to his old role. As months go by and Wallander does not come back to work there is a growing feeling that the illness will somehow turn into early retirement. There is much sadness in the Ystad police station as all levels of the staff know how much they relied on the ingenuity and enterprise of the inspirational inspector.

Wallander does go back to the office after he has worked all night to complete his detailed report on the murder of Louise Åkerblom and the whole catalogue of staggering events that followed it. He finds compiling the report a desperately difficult task, not least because he knows parts of it are not true. He keeps secret his bizarre collaboration with African killer Mabasha and he is astonished that none of his unconventional investigative acts are criticised by any of his colleagues. He decides this can only be because of the traditional police team spirit that is inclined to wrap a comforting corporate arm around any officer who has been compelled to take a life in the course of an operation.

After the bungling report is safely handed in, Wallander's depression is anything but eased. He knows that any real report on his behaviour throughout the investigation would describe how it was riddled with what he himself knows to be deep personal errors that he greatly regrets. It is a report he would never write but in his head he can read every word. Most importantly he knows he risked the life of his only daughter. Linda has generously assured her father many times that she does not blame him in any way for the terrible ordeal of being held in the cellar by the monstrous Konovalenko.

Some diversions do arrive in the form of an invitation to his father's wedding to his cheery home help, Gertrud, and both prospective partners appear delighted to have found such happiness in each other so late in life. Wallander is not at all sure whether he is in the right frame of mind to attend the ceremony. He spends some time writing a heartfelt letter to Baiba Leipa in Riga. He tries to explain his most intimate feelings to the woman he has fallen in love with and reveals that he may well have undertaken his last case as a policeman because he has finally decided he is unsuitable for the job.

Wallander does get a real lift when he finally returns to his repaired flat and finds a brand new stereo system along with a card from his workmates urging him to get well soon and hurry back to work. The generous surprise gift almost reduces Wallander to tears. It moves the detective deeply but his depression forces him to conclude that he does not really deserve such devotion.

The White Lioness was first published in Sweden in 1993 and an English translation did not appear until 1998. The *New York Times* raved about the book, calling it: 'Well paced... a thinking man's thriller.' But it was not until 2003 that John Lanchester in the *Daily Telegraph* favourably compared Wallander to Morse and other British detective favourites. He wrote: 'In prose as flat as the southern Swedish landscape, Henning Mankell has created a supremely satisfying detective series. Fictional detectives are grumpy. That is a rule of the genre, part of what makes even the darkest detective novel obscurely comfy. However gloomy and knackered we ourselves are, the man on the page is more so: Morse, Rebus, Dalgliesh. It would violate every propriety to have an imaginary copper who was well-rested and jolly, and who never thought about the job in his spare time. Inspector Kurt Wallander, the central character in *The White Lioness* and Henning Mankell's other detective novels, is very grumpy indeed – on a good day. On a bad day, he suffers from clinical depression. He is prone to melancholy, insomnia, nightmares, obsession, loneliness, overeating, diabetes; he is divorced; he has trouble communicating with his daughter, who lives far away in Stockholm; he has trouble communicating with his dying father; his relationships with women implode through gloom and inaction; he has no friends. And then, obviously, people around him start being murdered. Fantastic!'

Lanchester went on to make the point about the irritating order the *Wallander* stories were arriving in this country and offered some wise and perceptive advice. He said: 'One point of confusion is the sequence of the books. *The White Lioness* is the eighth Wallander novel to be translated, but it is the third in the sequence as it was written. (For fans: it's the one between *The Dogs of Riga* and *Sidetracked*.) This is one reason why I wouldn't recommend it as the place to start. Another reason is (and, as an admirer of the books, I feel I should murmur this sotto voce) that it's one of the least good of the Wallander novels.'

Wallander's troubles, however, are as compelling as ever – he goes from being down-in-the-mouth to outright mental – and there is one of the series' best villains, in the form of the ex-KGB man Konovalenko. The central chase sequence of the novel, with Wallander and Konovalenko trying to hunt each other, is excellent. Fans will be content with *The White Lioness*. For non-fans, or would-be fans, I think I would recommend one of the later books as a starting point: *Sidetracked*, perhaps, or *One Step Behind*. If you like them, go back to the beginning, start the sequence with *Faceless Killers*, and revel in the glorious luxury of not being a depressed Swedish police inspector.

CHAPTER SEVEN:

THE MAN WHO SMILED

The trauma suffered by Detective Chief Inspector Wallander during his lone crusade against the Russian villain Konovalenko as recounted in *The White Lioness* was much deeper than anyone imagined, including Wallander himself. He was out of action as a policeman for well over a year, convinced that his long and successful career was over. Taking away Wallander's job meant taking away the centre of his being. In all other areas of life he was pretty well universally useless and unhappy. His wife Mona had never regretted her decision to leave the self-confessed workaholic. While he accepted that theirs had never been a particularly happy marriage, Wallander still bitterly regretted her abrupt departure as he wallowed in his loneliness.

Battling depression and struck by a complete inability to work or even function normally, as the book begins he is signed off on long-term sick leave. Many observers must have considered that the policeman well known in Ystad, and a wider area beyond, for his integrity and dedication to duty was going completely off the rails. There seems to be no point to his life and Wallander grows more and more restive and unhappy. The cosy community of Ystad becomes almost claustrophobic to him at times and whenever he has some money to spare, he sets off on lone trips abroad, which generally end disastrously. In the hope of rediscovering his enthusiasm for the pleasures of life, he books a package visit to the beautiful Caribbean island of Barbados. But while surrounded by families of cheerful holidaymakers he feels miserable and sorry for himself from the start. He behaves stupidly from the moment the flight takes off and makes enormous use of the plane's bar on the outgoing journey. He steadily drinks himself into a gloom-laden stupor of oblivion. When he arrives, instead of simply relaxing, soaking up some sunshine and recharging his batteries, he feels nervous and withdrawn and stays in his hotel room for several days. He desperately wants to be on his own and refuses to have any contact with anyone else. He keeps clear of the beautiful beaches and only goes into the water once, when he falls over on a jetty and topples drunkenly into the sea.

When he does try to conquer his inability to have any social contact, he feels he has to fortify himself with so much booze beforehand that he has to go out and buy new supplies. Then he is approached by a local prostitute, which leads to a sickening spell of even more degrading depravity. Wallander's first reaction is to make it clear to the girl that he is not interested, but in his low mental state and befuddled by alcohol he succumbs to her charms. In fact, he stays with the prostitute for three days in her squalid home until she has separated him from all of his money, and then her two beefy brothers turn up and hurl him out on his ear. Wallander is unrecognisable from the highly principled, clear-thinking detective he once was. He is deeply disgusted with himself and slinks shame-facedly back to his hotel where he survives for the rest of his holiday on the breakfasts, which are included in his holiday deal. Back in Ystad his doctor warns him not to take any more such trips and makes it clear that he is in danger of losing his life to alcohol if he does not drastically reduce his drinking.

But Wallander is not in the mood for heeding advice, however sensible and well-intentioned it might be. He cannot afford to take another holiday so he borrows the money from his newly married father! For some time Wallander has steered clear of his elderly dad, who has just married a woman more than 30 years his junior. With nowhere else to turn for money, he approaches Povel pretending he wants to borrow the cash to buy some new furniture and cheer himself up. As soon as he gets the loan he goes instead to the local travel agency and books a three-week package trip to Thailand. There he drinks to obliterate his depression and also makes full use of the thriving sex industry. His already low self-image sinks almost out of sight as he sleeps with young prostitutes. He is heading for disaster until a fellow holidaymaker steps in. On the flight out Wallander had found himself sitting next to a retired pharmacist and the two men are staying at the same hotel. The pharmacist watches Wallander's self-destructive behaviour with horror. After he sees Wallander begin boozing at breakfast and acting more and more bizarrely, he takes action. Warning Wallander that he could have contracted a fatal disease, he packs the dysfunctional detective on a plane home a week early and very possibly saves his life. Wallander is desperately worried for months that he might have contracted a sexually transmitted disease but in the end he gets the all clear. By then he is so numbed by self-abuse that he scarcely reacts.

His daughter Linda returns from a trip to Italy and is shocked to discover what a sorry shape her father is in. She quickly pours away all his drink and forcefully informs him that he has to sort himself out. She stays for a fortnight at the flat in Mariagatan, and father and daughter become close again. By the time she leaves, Linda believes that her father has a reasonable chance of staying off the drink. Wallander knows deep down that Linda is right but he cannot face the prospect of moping round alone in his flat. So he books a room in a cheap guest house in the remote resort of Skagen in Jutland. It is a place where he had once been very happy. He and his wife Mona spent a holiday in Skagen soon after Linda was born, when the marriage was full of love and hope for the future. They were very hard up and were forced to live for a time in a leaking tent but they were content with their lot and optimistic about their future together.

This time around, Wallander spends his time going on long bicycle rides and keeps off the booze. He is trying to let his body recover from his horrendous solo drinking sessions and for the first time in many months he begins to sleep soundly at night.

Wallander writes to his sister Kristina and attempts to explain his emotions. He spells out how he feels ashamed and regretful that he has killed a man, even though it was in self-defence. He opens his heart to his sister and tries to convince her, and himself, that he can deal with the impact of the shocking deed. Then he writes to his old colleagues at Ystad police station, somewhat belatedly, thanking them for clubbing together and buying him the stereo system. He also says something he most certainly does not mean: that his health is improving and he is looking forward to coming back to work soon. In fact he is convinced his police career is over. He is sure he has lost the energy and the mental toughness to even consider a return to active service. He also writes to Baiba Leipa, the lady from Riga with whom he is now conducting a regular correspondence. He has deliberately played down the depth of his affection, and even love, for her. He is afraid that too frank and open an outline of his feelings will scare her off. At times he feels that any idea of building a life with Baiba is completely hopeless. After all, he had known her for only a few days at a time when she was shattered by the murder of the husband she loved. Certainly he helped her in her hour of need and even risked his life as he tried to right a terrible wrong, but he is still reluctant to open his heart too much in case his Latvian lover is altogether frightened off the whole daunting prospect of sharing her life with a caring but currently damaged Swedish policeman.

Day after day Wallander walks miles and miles on the lonely beaches, slowly rebuilding himself. He knows nothing and no one can be of any help to him at this time. Even his beloved opera is discarded and he listens instead to pop music with little depth, placing no demands on his troubled mind. As the months pass by he spends some time back home but always keeps returning to the little Skagen guest house. Very slowly his health improves. An absence of alcohol helps and the wall of depression begins to crumble just a little. But he is still sadly lacking confidence and riddled by self-doubt as he patrols the dunes and the beaches. He reflects that he is now in his late 40s and physically in better shape than he has enjoyed for years. Old clothes he had years ago grown out of now fit easily and he starts to think of his future. He considers retiring early from the police force and taking a job as a security guard. The prospect is not enticing and honest, law-abiding Wallander even considers embarking on a career breaking the laws he has fought so long and so hard to uphold. He knows of several police officers who have been tempted onto the wrong side of the law. Wallander tries to think of a get rich quick scheme that might leave him financially independent for the rest of his life. Quite quickly he comes to his senses and realises that he could never change. He recognises that he has a deeply ingrained sense of what is right and what is wrong that would never allow him to break the law. He wrestles for many weeks with the question of whether or not to attempt to go back to his job. He knows perfectly well that being a policeman has for many years been what made his life worth living. But now he feels that he has been so badly damaged by his experiences that he will not be able to do the job again.

Wallander feels a powerful surge of relief when he admits to himself that he will not return to the police force. He gets drunk in Skagen to celebrate his momentous decision. But then his peaceful idyll in the remote countryside is interrupted by a visitor. Wallander resents having his privacy invaded and is astonished to recognise Sten Torstensson, the lawyer who represented him in his long, painful and excruciatingly drawn out divorce proceedings. The two men had got on well in a difficult situation and Torstensson had taken Wallander sailing. Although the trip had been an unhappy experience for Wallander, who had vowed never to go on a sailing boat again, a friendship of sorts had developed. Yet Wallander is still very curious as to why the lawyer has gone to such considerable pains to track him down in his hideaway. Torstensson appeals to Wallander for help, both as a friend and as a policeman. The response is that Wallander is prepared to listen as a friend but he makes Torstensson the first to know of a momentous decision: he intends to resign from the police.

The lawyer is shocked by the news but ploughs on with a surprise of his own; his father is dead. He blurts out that Gustaf Torstensson has been killed in a road accident after a meeting with his most important client. The police have decided that Torstensson senior had simply been driving too fast in the fog and lost control and been killed as the car crashed. Sten is suspicious. He is convinced there is much more to his father's death than just a simple driving accident. He mentions a few unusual circumstances and Wallander listens, but then insists he can only be a friend and not a criminal investigator because he is no longer a police officer. The incident encourages Wallander to make the break from the force. He rings his old boss, Bjork, and tells him he has finally decided to leave. After a few days of relieved reflection that he has made the correct decision, he goes back home to Ystad to sign away the police career of which he was once so proud.

Having returned to his lonely flat he looks out on Mariagatan. He thinks deeply of the quarter of a century he has served as a policeman and he knows that, whatever happens to him next, this will always be the most important part of his life. He feels empty as he approaches his last day at work. Then he opens the local newspaper and sees details of a death notice that reads: 'Sten Torstensson, solicitor, born March 3 1947, died October 26, 1993.' At first Wallander cannot believe his eyes. Surely the man he had spoken to only a week previously cannot be dead? It must be a mistake, he thinks, a mix-up with his dead father. Briefly Wallander is completely poleaxed. He sits and thinks deeply for a while and then he does something he has not done for 18 months: rings one of his trusted old police colleagues,

Martinsson. The officer is delighted to hear from his long-time boss whose experience and insight he knows the force still sorely misses. And he gives Wallander the even more shocking news that Sten Torstensson was murdered, shot dead in his own office. Wallander realises his friend was killed very soon after making his appeal for help. Martinsson takes the opportunity to urge Wallander to come back to work and insists the Ystad force need him badly.

Wallander ends the call and replaces the receiver. He is stunned. In a few moments his resolution, made after 18 months of floundering around wondering what to do with his future, is thrown into question again. Wallander feels responsible and involved. He knows he turned Sten away in his hour of need and he now knows that he owes it to his friend to investigate. His decision to quit the police is instantly overturned in his head. Everything has changed. Wallander heads for the Ystad police station where Chief of Police Bjork is waiting reluctantly to accept his resignation. Bjork has the necessary papers ready when Wallander arrives. All it requires is a simple signature and his career in the police force is over, but Wallander shocks his old boss as he insists he will not be signing. He announces that he instead intends to resume his role. Bjork is delighted because although he did not always approve of Wallander's unorthodox methods he is the best detective he's ever known. Wallander has a single condition to his resumption; he wants to be in charge of investigating the Sten Torstensson case. That is no problem and Wallander is back in action. Bjork even admits it is the best piece of news he has heard in ages. Wallander demands his old office back and gets it. Ambitious Hanson, who had taken it over, is conveniently away on one of the many courses he goes on in order to increase his chances of promotion. Wallander is heartened to discover that although the desk has been changed, his familiar old chair remains. He sits down taking in all the atmosphere and aromas that he remembers so well. He is delighted to be back on duty.

There is just one surprise he is not quite sure how to react to. The little team of Bjork, Martinsson and Svedberg has acquired a new member, an attractive young woman called Ann-Britt Höglund. She is evidently a star recruit who was top of her class at police training college. Wallander is no misogynist but he muses instantly that a woman in the team changes everything. Svedberg is especially astonished by Wallander's return and blurts out in delight that they could not have managed another day without him. The room rings with laughter before the team settles down to tackle the curious case of two dead lawyers. Martinsson confides later to Wallander that they have missed him as much as they missed Chief Inspector Rydberg, who had died back in the spring of 1991. Rydberg had been Wallander's closest friend and now the returning detective feels daunted by the idea of taking his pal's place in the team's esteem. Martinsson sympathises with Wallander over his reaction to having killed a man. Wallander at last closes the door on the office he has regained. He feels flushed and hot with the underlying emotion of his return and takes his jacket and shirt off and wipes the sweat off his body with one of the curtains. Just as he is standing there half naked, Martinsson comes back in and is very shocked at the sight. Wallander tells him curtly to knock before entering next time. Clearly he wants to make it quite clear who is in charge.

Sten Torstensson was killed by someone who burst into his office and shot him three times. Clearly this was a deliberate, carefully planned murder. But Sten's father's death has been written off as a road accident and the police have discovered no link between the two deaths. Wallander is always reluctant to accept someone else's view of any set of occurrences so he resolves to start again on both investigations. A visit to the offices of both Torstenssons yields little information but near the scene of Gustaf's crash, Wallander finds a wooden chair leg that he hurls away in frustration. It is not until he later visits the wreck of the car in a scrapyard and finds the rest of the chair in the locked boot that Wallander instantly suspects foul play. He is furious about what seems like a very slipshod investigation that has too easily written off Torstensson Snr's death as a road accident. He is also furious because the scrapyard owner, a dubious character who has been the subject of several police inquiries, casually asks him what it is like to have killed somebody. Wallander angrily answers that it feels bloody awful. Back at the police station, he shows that he is back with a bang as he detonates a typical bombshell. With the team struggling to make any progress he tells them all flatly that Gustaf Torstensson did not die in a simple road accident. He was murdered, just like his son. And far from thinking the two cases are entirely separate, Wallander insists the two murders are clearly linked.

He leads the team back to the scene to find what he now knows might well be the murder weapon. He is irritated at having not realised the possible significance of the wooden chair leg on his first visit, though he blames poor detective work for not alerting him to the chair in the boot. Fortunately, they find the missing leg quite quickly and the team looks upon their returned leader with admiration. Wallander's great instinct for discovering vital clues is back on track and they are very happy about that. He himself is not sure he has made the right decision and he is not yet completely comfortable in his former role. He is still surprisingly shy of meeting other people and at his most content when on his own, even wondering to himself when this fear of being with people will finally subside. It requires a considerable effort of will simply to do his job when all the time he wants to be left alone. It is only then that Wallander reveals to the other detectives the meeting he had with Sten Torstensson in Skagen. They are stunned by the information and Bjork is clearly very upset that they are only now learning of Sten's heartfelt concerns about his father's death.

Wallander's re-integration into the team is not a painless process. He admits to Martinsson that he does not want to go round treading on people's toes but Martinsson thinks the increasing amount of bureaucracy that is coming into police work is much more of a problem. It takes a while but Wallander begins to feel that he is slowly regaining his old drive and energy. His memories of his squalid exploits in the Caribbean and in Thailand are pushed right to the back of his mind. The man who behaved like that was somebody he now feels he hardly knew. Mankell tells the reader that Wallander believes everyone has a 'secret room' somewhere in his or her psyche where all sorts of unpleasant memories are put away. Wallander now believes he had successfully stored away all of his awkward history and sealed it there for good. The day he is first convinced he has put his past behind him, he goes to the toilet and flushes away the anti-depressants he has been carrying around in his pocket like a mental life raft.

The investigation soon uncovers that, although he had once had many clients, in the period leading up to his untimely death Gustaf Torstensson worked almost exclusively for a super-rich Swedish businessman called Alfred Harderberg, who lives in some splendour in fabulous Farnholm Castle. This mysterious, rarely photographed tycoon is said to have an aquarium with genuine gold dust at the bottom instead of sand. Gustaf was driving home from a meeting with Harderberg the night he died, so naturally Wallander is keen to interview him as soon as possible. However, he is interrupted by a rare call from his father, ringing to ask his son why he never gets in touch. Wallander has not told his father he has decided to go back to work. He reflects that he has been in the police for more than 25 years and throughout that time his father never missed an opportunity to criticise his choice of work. He realises his father is owed at least an explanation and promises to visit him.

Wallander is still far from confident. Often he feels very uneasy about his solitary state and he consoles himself by having long, imaginary conversations with Baiba Leipa, as though she were with him in Ystad rather than miles away in Riga. But all too often the image of the woman he loved fades, and the familiar sight of himself scrambling around with guns in both hands and a man being shot in the head returns to trouble him. It is a desperately miserable memory that continues to haunt him. He thinks to himself that he is a man who simply does not laugh often enough. There is very little humour or lightness in his life. Mankell cleverly gives the reader so much enthralling detail of the detective's mental processes that we get a real insight into the lonely world of Wallander as he struggles to restart his precious career. He drives home and cooks a forgettable meal, waters his five plants, fills the washing machine with clothes that have been littered around the flat, then finds he has no washing powder so sits sadly on the sofa and cuts his toenails. The picture the book so brilliantly paints is of a desperately sad and solitary man who only really comes to life when he is unravelling a complex mystery. It's almost impossible not to sympathise with the detective with so little to cheer about in his private life. Yet Wallander somehow never sinks into self-pity and instead drives himself on to solve whatever intrigue-wrapped villainy is set before him.

At Farnholm Castle he meets a disgraced ex-policeman

who is in charge of security and a smooth talking secretary who deflects all his questions. Mr Harderberg is irritatingly elusive, having flown out of the country in his private jet on business. No sooner is that frustrating visit over than Wallander is called by the Torstensson's terrified secretary, Mrs Duner, who reports that someone has been in her garden in the night. Wallander answers the call and finds that a land mine has been planted in her lawn! Wallander explodes it with the aid of a hurled telephone directory and realises that the people he is up against are quite prepared to wipe out anyone who threatens them. Wallander is depressed by the ever-increasing violence. He never thought he would see the day when he detected a land mine in a Ystad garden.

Wallander is in the middle of another compelling investigation and successfully starting to shed his depression. Nonetheless, he is intrigued when Per Akeson, the prosecutor, reveals his own escape route from the run-of-the-mill round of working for Swedish justice. Akeson, who remarks that he is about the same age as Wallander, has applied for a United Nations legal post and is hoping to land a two-year contract in Uganda. He says something that resonates with Wallander; that he woke up one morning and wondered if there might be more to life than his routine role. Wallander advises Akeson to jump at the job if he gets the chance, but it is clearly not something he would do himself.

Ann-Britt Höglund sometimes has to take time off work to care for her children and some of the male officers clearly think she is doing a job that would be better done by a male officer. But Wallander does not share this opinion. He is quickly impressed by Höglund's keen brain and the two head off together to investigate a lead on a trip that almost costs them their lives. Höglund notices that they are being followed as they drive to their destination. When they stop and pretend to get petrol they seem to lose their 'tail' but later Wallander realises they left the car unguarded and suspects it has been tampered with. He stops on the main road and insists Höglund come well away from the vehicle. She is not happy because she's left her handbag inside but Wallander's instinct for detecting danger proves invaluable as the car spectacularly explodes by the roadside. Afterwards Wallander wonders whether Höglund noticed how frightened he had become. On the surface he has played the role of experienced police officer, taking control in difficult circumstances, but underneath he had been shaking with fear that he had brought a young woman into such peril. He had wished with all his heart that he was alone in the car.

Wallander's relationship with Höglund is at times difficult and strained as her character is sometimes used by Mankell to symbolise the changing times that the aging detective finds so disturbing and uncomfortable. He quickly recognises her sharp intelligence and takes her into his confidence, perhaps more so than with far more experienced officers like Martinsson and Svedberg. But he resists the role of male protector and feels instantly uneasy whenever situations push him in that direction.

He is also swiftly irritated when Höglund fails to take on board snippets of hard-earned wisdom about the job. Wallander is very fond of recalling some of the sayings of his old, dead friend Rydberg. At one point, when Höglund is despairing that they are not acquiring knowledge and information quickly enough, Wallander tells her that Rydberg, who was a 'wise bird', once said that police officers always tend to say they know nothing, while in fact they often know more than they think. Wallander is pleased with this gem and believes it to be true so he is annoyed and deflated when Höglund responds that it sounds like the sort of thing they were told at police training college and instantly forgot about. Wallander sharply tells her that she should listen to what he has to say. She could learn a great deal from Rydberg and indeed from him.

Wallander perseveres with his attempts to explain some of the aspects of everyday policing that she has not been able to learn in her lectures at college. He certainly opens up on his feelings about how crime has changed even in a sleepy little seaside town like Ystad. He shares his fears over the way life has become more violent and nasty and how standards of behaviour have fallen during his working lifetime. Respect for the police has slipped steadily and the resources which the police have to deal with the ever-growing numbers of crimes are still severely restricted. Wallander feels aggrieved that often less serious crimes are simply ignored because the police do not have the time or manpower to deal with them. But he is able to joke that if murder becomes a crime that is left undetected, then the police will have to rise up and mutiny. He tells Höglund the best time to stage an uprising would be when the police commissioner was out of the country eating posh dinners in the name of public relations.

Dealing with criminals who are clearly both well-organised and ruthless certainly concentrates Wallander's mind. It soon becomes clear to him that Alfred Harderberg is the man behind the killings. The elusive billionaire is at the centre of a string of dodgy dealings that are both large-scale and difficult to prove. Wallander concludes that Gustaf Torstensson was terminated because he knew too much and his son Sten was murdered because he began investigating his father's death. Wallander is anxious to proceed very carefully. Any criminal callous enough to plot and carry out killings on such a scale deserves to be stalked and hunted as warily as possible.

But just as the police investigation intensifies, Wallander gets a visit from Svedberg with news of a personal problem that requires his immediate attention. His elderly father has been arrested for fighting! Wallander rushes over to the small town of Simrishamn, where his father has turned violent in an off-licence. On this journey, Mankell gives the reader a fascinating insight into Wallander's childhood. The detective thinks back to when he was 11 years old – the last time his father was arrested. Mankell is very careful in deciding exactly how much of Wallander's distinctive upbringing he shares but these particular memories tell us a great deal about the character of the man. Wallander recalls a Saturday back in 1956 when some of his father's 'glamorous' friends turned up at their house in their smart clothes. He secretly kept a diary and recorded how these men had big hats and wore huge rings on their fingers. They would bargain with his father over his paintings and then banknotes would be flamboyantly peeled from enormous wads. The negotiations would always be lubricated with generous slurps of brandy and eventually his father would happily pocket the money. The young Wallander formed a very romantic image in his mind of these visitors and he privately called them the Silk Knights.

Sometimes he would be given some small change for helping to carry the purchased paintings to the men's car. And he remembers vividly that as the men drove away into the distance his father's jolly mood would vanish and he would spit after the visitors and snarl that again he had been cheated. The young Wallander could not understand how his father could be unsatisfied by what looked like bundles of money in exchange for copies of the same Swedish landscape, sometimes with a grouse and other times without. Mankell dryly calls it: 'A landscape illuminated by a sun that was never allowed to set.' Wallander remembers just one painting sale that ended differently. That time, two men he had never seen before came to make the purchase. After the deal was struck the men suggested they all went for something to eat. Wallander and his father climbed into the car and the adults went to a restaurant while young Kurt was handed some small change and sent to play on the roundabouts in the park. Wallander could see his father and the men eating their meal in the distance and noted that after food, lots of bottles and glasses filled the table. As afternoon turned into evening a huge commotion broke out in the restaurant. Wallander rushed over as a small crowd gathered to see his father at the centre of a huge fight with one of the two men. Security guards were attempting to break it up. The table was turned over and glasses and bottles were smashed in the melee. Police appeared and his father and the two men were dragged away. Wallander cried as he saw his father driven away in a police car. He walked all the way home in the rain and sat all night in his father's studio.

His father was very upset that his son had been abandoned. Even in his inebriated and angry state he had told the police to take care of his young boy but he had been ignored. Wallander was moved to hear his father apologise. The spark for the dust up is another wonderful illustration of Mankell's delicious humour, which gently underpins so many of the stories. Wallander's father and the two men had been arguing about the bird that was present in many of the paintings. Wallander's father had painted a grouse but the two men had insisted it was a partridge! Kurt consoled his father by agreeing that the bird was obviously a grouse and added that anyone could see it was not a partridge. His father rewarded him with a beaming smile which revealed that two of his front teeth were missing since the fight. Kurt thought sadly that his father's smile 'was broken'. There had been a moderately happy ending to the story as the two men remained friends and customers of Wallander's father. One of them even paid his daunting dental bill.

This poignant childhood memory is re-run as Wallander drives to Simrishamn to sort out the latest mess his father has got himself into. He discovers that his father had travelled by taxi to the off licence, where customers were given tickets so that they were served in turn. Wallander's father missed his turn and later went up to the counter and demanded to be served. The assistant insisted he get a new ticket and start again at the back of the queue. Another customer, whose turn had just arrived, pushed past and told Wallander's father to get lost. He, despite his age and obvious frailty, promptly thumped the man. The shop assistant intervened and Wallander's father thumped him as well.

Wallander finds his father in a police cell and drives him home, still angrily protesting that he was perfectly within his rights to defend himself. Gradually the old man calms down and the two men enjoy a rare intimate moment as they recall the earlier incident. But Wallander Snr is adamant that he was justified in lashing out to preserve his dignity. He asks his son not to mention anything to his new wife, Gertrud, who has apparently sparked such a big improvement in Wallander's father's health and lifestyle. Kurt muses gloomily that deep down he does not really know his father very well and, equally, his father does not know him either. Wallander Snr was always set against his son entering the police force and working as a detective, and his opinion has not changed with age. The encounter ends warmly with Kurt confiding to his father that he used to call the art dealers who visited all those years ago the 'Silk Knights'. Wallander's father clearly approves of the name and the men part on good terms for once. But as he drives back home, Kurt tries without any success to work out what it is about his inherently decent but frequently dysfunctional father that reminds him so much of himself.

The great narrative drive soon takes over and Mankell's ability for setting his books against a realistic background gives British readers a jolt when they read that the deadly and unscrupulous villain whom Wallander is investigating was once an associate of one Robert Maxwell, who fell to his death from his yacht some two years earlier. Mankell's sinister figure of Alfred Harderberg turns out to have been closely linked to the monstrous and all too real Maxwell. Harderberg, of course, is fictional but even before the reader gets to meet him, he is totally believable. Wallander is increasingly troubled as he discovers the extraordinary extent of the web of Harderberg's criminal activities that are so cleverly clothed in the respectable appearance of one of the country's leading businessmen. Like many Swedes, Wallander has grown up believing in the basic integrity of Swedish business practices. Other nationalities might throw up flawed tycoons on a terrifying scale but surely the great Swedish business success, which is at the root of the country's status in the world, must be based on honesty? Wallander wonders why that honesty is so unquestioned. The thriving export industry is so fundamental to the nation's prosperity that it takes some time for Wallander to appreciate the extent of Harderberg's ruthlessness. Mankell uses youthful and intelligent Ann-Britt Höglund to help alert Wallander to the scale of what they are up against. She knows a financial whizz kid who unearths Harderberg's link to dirty deeds and she reminds Wallander that they need to investigate deep underneath the shiny corporate facades of outwardly upright and correct businesses.

When Höglund spells out to Wallander that in order to find out who killed the Torstenssons (and who tried to kill them by blowing up the car), they will have to ruffle a few feathers in the business world, he knows she is telling the truth. With the challenging enthusiasm of youth, she insists that even noble families have some crooks in their ranks. Wallander says he had not thought of it like that but he muses to himself that, in fact, he knows what she is saying is correct. He knows his generation of police officers has not always tackled crime in high and important places as rigorously as they might have done. And he does not particularly enjoy the experience of being reminded of his own shortcomings by this bright, young policewoman. Wallander realises that with his massive resources, Harderberg most probably has spies within the police force. He knows if he openly turns the investigation in his direction, Harderberg will know long enough in advance to take effective action to avoid the danger of arrest and discovery. So Wallander tells the trusted members of his team that while

Harderberg is undoubtedly their target, they are going to proceed in a manner that does not give that decision away. Höglund impresses Wallander at this time as she is always quick to point out weaknesses in his strategy and helpful enough to come up with improvements. Without a hint of any physical attraction between the two officers, Wallander and Höglund become close at this planning stage of their operation. They both feel frustrated by the growing amount of bureaucracy that gets in the way of the more important part of their jobs and at one point Höglund laughs that perhaps they are in the wrong job. Not the wrong job, replies Wallander. 'But maybe we're living at the wrong time,' he adds thoughtfully.

Mankell hands the reader the fascinating background information that the impact of the unsuccessful investigation into the killing of Swedish Prime Minister Olof Palme some ten years earlier continues to be felt strongly by the forces of law and order. Police bungling is still blamed for not finding the assassin, as certain officers were criticised for not identifying the right suspect before launching into action. As Wallander asks Akeson for the go-ahead to focus on Harderberg, he also angrily tackles his boss Bjork, whom he has discovered had warned the businessman of the police investigation. Bjork insists it was purely politeness to 'an important man in our society'. Wallander realises then exactly what he is up against. At the back of his mind he also feels very guilty for dismissing his friend Sten Torstensson in his hour of need. He was at such a low point in his personal life at the time that he had not found himself able to do anything but turn the lawyer away. This guilt gnaws at him and the investigation becomes something of a private crusade.

Martinsson cynically suggests that a really complex murder case was all it took to bring Wallander back to health and back to action, and the others nod in agreement at the thought. The small team works long hours to build up as much information as possible on Harderberg and his intricate financial fortress. They find enough details of crooked deals and mysterious suicides of awkward colleagues and business rivals to convince all members of the team that they are on the right track. Wallander again visits sinister Farnholm Castle and interviews Harderberg face to face. The billionaire appears friendly and says he can't imagine who would want to kill Gustaf Torstensson. But there is something about his ever present smile, which gives the book its title, and the replies to particular questions that convinces Wallander that, beyond any doubt, he is their man.

The police make a breakthrough when the strange plastic container found in Gustaf Torstensson's car the night he was murdered is identified as one used for transporting body parts intended for transplants. All of a sudden Wallander digs up details of a chillingly evil illicit trade in body parts, linking up with gangs in South America and Asia who commit murders simply to sell organs from the corpses of their victims. Wallander is struck by the outrageous thought that this elderly solicitor had discovered that Harderberg's business empire included this vile trade and had stolen the container to use as evidence of what was going on. It is a shattering accusation but there is no evidence to back it up. Wallander and his fellow detective debate for hours on their next move as they desperately attempt to find out more information about Harderberg. As the case stalls Wallander suffers from horrendous nightmares. One involves the death of his father and when he rushes to look in his coffin, it is his daughter Linda lying there dead instead.

The challenge faced by his small team to penetrate the carefully-laid defences of a vastly rich international organisation suddenly seems to weigh very heavily on the once intrepid Detective Chief Inspector. He is pressured by Bjork and Akeson to get results quickly and finds he is beginning to lose his newly restored confidence. He thinks to himself that he has lost his grip and should hand over the investigation to someone else. He knows he looks as bad as he feels when kind-hearted Ebba asks who he thinks will thank him if he works himself to death. But a chance to pierce the strict security at Farnholm Castle arrives with the publication of an advertisement in the local paper for the job of stable girl. Wallander realises if he could get someone he can trust inside the Castle he might have a chance of lowering the odds on success. He rings his friend, Sten Widen. Their youthful friendship had been somewhat revived after Wallander involved him in the shattering adventure that was *The White Lioness*. Now Widen is understandably wary of his old friend's approach and he is initially horrified when he discovers that Wallander wants one of his stable girls to be a spy in the Castle. But he is eventually persuaded to help out.

Wallander is always open-minded and prepared to go to any lengths to get the information he is searching for. He approaches an investigative journalist who has been digging around in the murky world of murderous body-part dealers. Wallander is shocked to learn the facts of this grim sort of life. The journalist tells Wallander of the ease of having someone killed in the slums of big cities like Rio or Lagos or Calcutta. It evidently takes only a fee of 20 or 30 dollars to find an efficient hit man and another set of organs is there for lucrative disposal. He is disturbed about yet more details of the cheapness of human life and the depravity of some criminals. If there is a Swedish link to this dreadful trade he is more than ever determined to deal with it.

No one can accuse Kurt Wallander of not experiencing ordinary human emotions like fear. When he realises that someone had been inside his apartment and that two guys are outside in a car apparently watching him, he is absolutely terrified. He sneaks out of the apartment the back way and runs to the home of his colleague, Svedberg. Together they confirm that Wallander's fears are justified but Wallander insists on dealing with the menace himself. When he discovers from his stable girl spy that Harderberg is making plans to leave his Castle, Wallander realises time is running out. He decides to go alone into the Castle. His only concession to his own personal safety is to have Ann-Britt Höglund in contact by telephone from outside the grounds. Wallander is shocked to discover the body of Harderberg's ex-police security boss and he is even more surprised when he is dazzled by a bright light. He is easily captured, overpowered and knocked unconscious. When he comes round he is forced to listen to Harderberg, who is no longer smiling but telling him he is to be dropped to his certain death out of a helicopter. It seems that the villain is going to get away. But, in some captivating action scenes, Wallander manages to outwit his two guards and then race against time to stop Harderberg fleeing the country. In dramatic action sequences at the local airport Wallander just manages to stop the arch villain's plane taking off.

The book ends with Kurt Wallander totally restored to his role as Ystad's premier crime-fighter. Yet it still seems he is destined to have a lonely life. It is Christmas Eve when he heads for the airport to greet what for the reader is a surprise visitor. Baiba Leipa arrives to join Wallander in Ystad and we are left wondering if our hero has perhaps at last found happiness.

The Man Who Smiled was first published in Sweden in 1994. It was not published in Britain in translation until 2005. *The Times* rated it simply as: 'One of the best... absorbing, chilling and dripping with evil atmosphere.' In the *Sydney Morning Herald*, Ian Hicks wrote: 'If you can hear the sound of heartfelt cheers echoing through the book world, don't be surprised. The hosannas come from the followers of Henning Mankell, the Swedish writer of nine police procedural novels featuring the dour

Detective Chief Inspector Kurt Wallander. And why are they cheering? They are welcoming the arrival – at last – of *The Man Who Smiled*. It is 11 years since the book, the fourth in the series, was first published in Sweden. Just why it has taken more than a decade to reach Britain and Australia (it has not yet been published in the US and Canada) is a mystery worthy of Wallander's immediate attention... the question, of course, is: was it worth the wait? Indeed it was. Mankell's yarn is a beauty which fits well into the painstaking development of Kurt Wallander as a realistic character, quite the equal of Michael Dibdin's Aurelio Zen, Ian Rankin's John Rebus or Donna Leon's Guido Brunetti. And, as was the case in earlier Wallander fictions, Mankell has been well served by his translator. We, the readers, know who the criminal is from the very first pages of the book. Our enjoyment comes from watching Wallander and his team painstakingly put the puzzle together for themselves. If we are going to take Wallander seriously as a character we need to know why he is the gruff, injudicious loner who makes such a violent impact in the second half of Mankell's series. In the third book of the series, Wallander has killed a man in the line of duty; in the fifth he has become a hard man who takes little for granted and less at face value. In the fourth, the fictional missing link, we meet Wallander not in his familiar patch at Ystad on the southern tip of Sweden but on a desolate, windswept beach in Denmark. Having shot a man dead, Wallander tries but fails to lose himself in alcohol, unsafe sex and a bottomless pit of self-pity. Having decided to leave the police force, he spurns a plea for help from an old friend whose father has died in a car crash that is no accident. Then he sees the friend himself murdered. Stung at long last into action, he will do more than merely catch the man responsible; he will also lose all faith in the worth of modern Swedish society and in its most cherished institutions. *The Man Who Smiled* is more than a dreadful trudge through the worst our modern world has to offer. There is always Mankell's leavening of humanity and his thoughtful, dry humour. There's also a nice word picture of the next generation of police in the person of Ann-Britt Höglund, a beauty with a brain in blue blouse and jeans.'

CHAPTER EIGHT:
SIDETRACKED

In all the wonderful *Wallander* adventures, the most memorable image, in the books and on the screen, is surely the sight of a terrified and traumatised teenage girl setting fire to herself in a field of rape seed. As our hero strides out through the billowing yellow sea of the crop to help the unknown young woman, he tries to reassure her by calling out that he is 'police'. In a scene that is deeply shocking, she pours petrol over her head, strikes a lighter and incinerates herself. It's hideously unforgettable and it begins what for this reader is perhaps the most enthralling *Wallander* story of them all.

It was no great surprise that the BBC chose to launch their first series of *Wallander* films with *Sidetracked*. Kenneth Branagh is simply compelling and totally convincing in just about every second of his portrayal of Kurt Wallander but he is never better than when he is conveying his own appalled reaction to this terrible waste of a life that introduces the story. The BBC film is my favourite of the six screened so far, and remarkably it manages to bring to viewers a good deal of the extraordinary detail of the 500 pages of the scintillating novel. The memorable story is one of a teenage boy taking ruthless, yet richly deserved, revenge on rich men who ruined the life of his sister and other young women through their sickening sexual depravity.

The book begins with Wallander forced to make a speech to mark Bjork's retirement as Chief of Police in Ystad. Wallander reflects to himself that he would much rather be speaking up against the looming cutbacks and reorganisations which everyone in the force knows will leave the police thinner on the ground to deal with the ever-rising crime levels. There are rumours that much police work is to be outsourced to security companies. Wallander is also some way from overjoyed that the intellectually limited Hansson has been appointed Acting Chief. Not that Wallander ever wanted the job for himself, but Hansson had never been one of the brightest or more imaginative officers.

Sidetracked in print is set against another backdrop which irritates Wallander, the 1994 World Cup. Kurt has very little interest in football, even with Sweden involved, and he is bewildered by the bizarre grip the competition appears to have on the rest of the nation.

Wallander is looking forward to going off on a short holiday with Baiba and he is surprised to learn that promising young detective Ann-Britt Höglund knows all about what he thought was his secret relationship with the Latvian policeman's widow. Ann-Britt laughs that all his police colleagues know about the new woman in his life and jokes that it has been the subject of an 'ongoing internal investigation'. Wallander is stunned. His relationship with Baiba is indeed very new but she has already pulled him out of the crippling depression he fell into after his wife Mona left him. Baiba came to Ystad to stay with him at Christmas and he has spent time in Riga with her. Now they are planning a holiday in Skagen in Denmark. Wallander is very fond of Baiba but he prefers to keep his private life private. He wants to get married but Baiba values her freedom very highly and is unwilling to commit herself to becoming a wife again so soon. Meanwhile, the behaviour of Wallander's headstrong daughter Linda is also troubling him. She announces that she has abandoned her plans for a career in furniture restoration and is now preparing to put on some kind of stage performance with a girlfriend. Wallander is not enthusiastic, and he is also concerned that he has not seen Linda for some time.

The terrible shock at the start of the story comes when Wallander goes out to check on a call from a farmer about a strange woman standing in the middle of a rape field. As he strides towards her she pours petrol over herself and sets it on fire. On screen it is shattering and, even as Mankell tells it in the book, it is one of those chilling sequences that really disturbs the reader. Wallander is devastated and turns away to be violently sick. Afterwards he cannot get the image of the dying girl out of his head for months. He is simply shattered to be living in a world where a young person can take her own life right in front of him.

Of course, as always, there is much more going on in Wallander's life in the book than can be conveyed in 90 minutes of screen time. We read about Wallander operating against a growing pattern of disaffection from his fellow law-upholding professionals. Prosecutor Per Akeson asks Wallander for advice on how he should break it to his wife that he has secured a year's sabbatical working for the United Nations with refugees in Uganda. His wife will most definitely be staying at home, and he can't think how to tell her. Wallander has no advice to give but he feels desperately jealous. He wishes he and Baiba could go off together to Uganda, or somewhere else exotic, and forget all about Ystad and police work for a while. He wonders if he has really recovered from the depression that put him out of action for 18 months after he shot a man dead. His mood hardly improves when his sister Kristina criticises him for not spending more time visiting their father. Wallander resents her remarks and hates the way she reminds him of their mother, who died years earlier from cancer. He remembers when he was young that it always seemed to be a battle of the sexes in the Wallander household, Kristina and their mother up against him and his father. Young Kurt never had a very happy relationship with his mother, which is another parallel with the author.

The death of the young girl continues to trouble Wallander. He talks to the doctor who has looked at the charred body. She thinks the girl was just 15 years old.

Wallander is mortified. He can't believe anyone so young could do such a thing to herself and that it is not exceptionally extraordinary behaviour, but the doctor tells him about a seven-year-old girl who deliberately blew herself up and about a four-year-old boy who attempted to poke his own eyes out because he was afraid of his father. The doctor confirms Wallander's fears that death by burning is one of the most excruciating ways to go and by the end of the conversation he is close to despair. But just as he heads off to see his father, news comes in of another shocking death. The former Minister of Justice, Gustaf Wetterstedt, has been found murdered and it looks as if he has been scalped! The retired Minister had been unpopular with the police and there had been hints of a scandal about his private life but nothing had ever come to court. There is no way Wallander can visit his father as planned now and, although he knows he should telephone and explain himself, he asks Ann-Britt Höglund to do it for him and to pretend she is the Chief of Police if his father asks.

The importance of the latest murder victim has some police officers behaving very nervously. Acting Chief Hansson is particularly anxious not to make any mistakes. He reminds Wallander that it is ten years since the Swedish Prime Minister was murdered and that particular police investigation was later described as disastrous. He doesn't want to take responsibility and is keen for Per Akeson to contact the chief public prosecutor. Wallander is not impressed by Hansson's obvious lack of confidence and feel for command.

Wallander finds pornographic pictures at Wetterstedt's home and he discovers from a drunken, old journalist friend that the ex-Minister was a vile sleazeball and a key member of a secret organisation that callously imports pretty young girls purely for the perverted sexual needs of groups of dirty, very rich and well-connected old men. Wallander is outraged but just as he is attempting to concentrate on the complex investigation, his father makes his first ever visit to the police station, with shattering news. Wallander is furious when a girl in reception allows his father to wait in his office, but when his father reveals that he has been diagnosed with Alzheimer's all of Wallander's emotions change instantly. In a very downbeat and matter of fact way, his father, who can't recall the name of the illness, says: 'I'm starting to lose my mind. It's a disease with a name I can't remember. It's like getting senile but it can make you angry at everything and it can progress very fast.'

Wallander is shattered. He feels desperately sorry for his father and wishes that they had been closer during the past years. But Wallander's father is not in the police station for sympathy. He wants help from his son to realise one of his long-held ambitions while he still has the ability to appreciate it. Wallander is deeply moved as his father comes close to begging him to go on a trip to Italy. The old man says he has the money to pay for it and Wallander sees how frail and elderly his father has become. He agrees instantly to go and they decide on a week in September. Once the expedition is firmly agreed, Wallander's father heads off briskly, saying: 'You never know. The trip might be fun!' Meanwhile, Wallander himself is reduced to tears. He is supposed to be a razor-sharp and dedicated detective in charge of a complex and shocking murder investigation but he is reduced to an emotional wreck. Even though his relationship with his father has long been difficult and strained, he feels guilty that they are not closer and is completely overwhelmed when his father turns to him for help in his hour of need. The prospect of his father slowly losing his wits is desperately grim. He resolves that nothing will stand in the way of taking his father to Italy. The impact of his father's illness and the pressure of his demanding job weighs heavily on Wallander.

A second apparently eminent citizen with a private enthusiasm for young girls is axed to death and scalped. At a police press conference Wallander becomes irritated by a persistent reporter until he bangs on a table and shouts that he will not let the investigation be influenced by a journalist who does not know when to stop asking questions. The angry outburst makes news itself and Wallander receives a phone call from the national police board criticising his behaviour.

Wallander's mood is lifted when Linda comes to visit with her new friend and theatrical partner, Kajsa. He is disappointed that she is not going ahead with her idea of settling down in Ystad as a theatrical restorer. He always seems to be surprised by women and he certainly is the next day when a murder victim's daughter slaps him hard across the face. She is frustrated that the hunt for her father's killer appears to be getting nowhere. Wallander is stunned and he thinks of a previous interview when a man suspected of burglary suddenly thumped him in the face. That time Wallander struck back so hard that he broke the man's nose. The man tried to sue for police brutality but lost. But Wallander had never been hit by a woman before, although he recalls to himself that his wife Mona used to throw things at him occasionally. He wonders whether he would have hit her back if she had lashed out and he knows there is a good chance he would have done.

Wallander is hit by another surprise outpouring of emotion in a phone call from his sister Kristina. She has spoken to Gertrud, his father's wife, and she is distraught at the diagnosis of Alzheimer's. Wallander attempts to comfort Kristina and insists he will take their father to Italy as he wishes. Kristina offers to come too, but Wallander says the trip is just for him and their father. Wallander tries to break the news about the old man's illness as gently as possible to his granddaughter but Linda is still deeply upset. He attempts to explain how her grandfather's personality might change as Alzheimer's takes hold of him. They visit Löderup, where Wallander Snr and Gertrud live, and it is a very difficult occasion for Kurt. The trip to Italy is the only thing the old man talks about, says Gertrud, and Wallander and Linda stay to eat dinner in the garden. Wallander's life has very few family get-togethers in it. He is a very solitary man for most of the time but he enjoys this occasion greatly, even though it is sparked by such sad news. Linda tells her father he is becoming more and more like the old man and he says he knows, but he is not sure if he likes it. Remarkably, out of this intimate moment comes an inspiration for his investigation. Linda says 'adults can be so childlike' and later the comment registers with Wallander, who rushes back to one of the crime scenes and retrieves a comic that he had disregarded earlier. It turns out to be a key piece of evidence.

Wallander's relationship with Baiba is very fragile at this time. Each time they speak on the phone he fears that she is going to tell him it is all over between them. Wallander's anxiety levels build to almost unbearable levels as he sees that what he feels might be his chance of personal happiness hangs by a thread. He worries about Baiba, about his job, even about mundane events like his car breaking down. He wonders if the psychological profiler the police have brought in to help solve the murder case might not also do a report on himself, to come up with a solution to his endless worrying. He is buried so deeply in his work that the underlying loneliness of his life is hard to shake off. He has a very unprofessional penchant for being attracted to women he meets in the course of his work, particularly ones who are hopelessly inappropriate. The investigation leads him to interview a female vicar at Helsingborg who turns out to be a very beautiful woman. Wallander can't help fantasising about her and, in fact, it leads him to track down an important witness. It is a vital breakthrough even if the thought processes appear highly unprofessional. Later Wallander has an erotic dream featuring the lady vicar that surprises him and makes him feel a little ashamed

Sidetracked tells an enthralling story of some of Sweden's most powerful and eminent citizens callously abusing their positions in society to use and abuse innocent and helpless young girls. The plight of the vulnerable victims angers Wallander and drives him on to work harder than ever. As the story unfolds, Mankell cannot resist a little social comment and has a wise old public servant explain to Wallander that a change of attitude took place at some time in the 1950s. The suggestion is that while on the surface it seemed that increasing prosperity was bringing Sweden the ability to obliterate poverty and raise living standards, there was a corresponding reduction in standards of behaviour from politicians and public servants. Mankell spells it out: 'Idealism had been a dominant force in public life but this idealism became diluted.'

Wallander is concerned that despite the claims that wealth is growing for all, in reality the gap between rich and poor in Sweden is widening rather than narrowing. After searching the homes of two affluent victims of the killer, he has to do a similar job on the house of one of the brutal heavies employed by the criminal organisation. It is like a filthy rubbish tip and Wallander reflects that this is what his country is like nowadays, and concludes to himself: 'The differences between people are just as great now as they were when some lived in manor houses and others in hovels.'

Wallander's daughter Linda stays with her father and

the pair sit up half the night talking. He is pleased to realise that she is an adult now and not simply his little girl. But she breaks the news to her father that her mother Mona has been talking about getting married again and Wallander again becomes depressed. Linda asks him about his own new relationship with Baiba and he tries to explain how delicate and uncertain things are between the two of them. He is pleased to realise that Linda does not blame him for splitting up with her mother and that she understands that the break-up had been 'necessary'.

The deep-thinking session appears to spark Wallander to muse on the difficult case in hand and also on changes in Swedish society. Mankell reveals some of his own concerns through Wallander's musings on how much things have changed. Although he knows his nation has become much more affluent, Wallander himself cannot remember any real poverty in his youth. But he is concerned about 'spiritual poverty' and a decline in the importance of the family unit. Mankell opens up Wallander's thoughts to the reader when he muses: 'When we got rid of the old society where families stuck together, we forgot to replace it with something else. The great loneliness that resulted was a price we didn't know we were going to have to pay. Or perhaps we chose to ignore it.'

Just when he is desperately trying to concentrate on the bewildering case, he receives an anguished call from Gertrud. She is distraught because Kurt's father appears to have taken leave of his senses and is burning his paintings. Wallander rushes over and finds his father looking wild and demented, and apparently set on torching his studio and everything inside it. Wallander has to shoulder the door open and gently coax his father out of his angry rage. Eventually the old man calms down and looks around at the mess he has made as if he has no idea what has happened. Wallander feels desperately sorry for his father as he sees the effects of his illness. But the old man goes for a lie down and seems back to his normal self. Gertrud thinks this behaviour means that the trip to Rome planned for September will have to be cancelled but Wallander insists he will look after his father so long as his father still wants to make the trip and remains physically capable.

The killings continue and the reader knows that the murderer is the remarkable 14-year-old brother of a girl who is in a mental institution after being used and abused by sick and sadistic predators. The boy uses some shocking violence, hammering an axe through the skull of one man and pouring hydrochloric acid into the eyes of his cruel father, who is an employee of the vile gang. Astonishingly, fingerprints found on his father's eyelids are among the clues that help Wallander to realise that this young revenge-seeking son is capable of these terrible crimes. Justice moves very slowly and a particularly evil businessman who has cruelly treated young girls ends his days butchered, his head roasted to a crisp in an oven.

Wallander slowly tightens the net around the resourceful young killer. He is supposed to be heading off on holiday to Skagen in Denmark with Baiba in a few days time but stubbornly refuses to warn her that he might not be able to make it. In the end he turns, very unprofessionally as he admits to himself, to colleague Ann-Britt who offers to ring and explain. After some highly dramatic sequences, Wallander finally captures the teenage terminator, just in time to meet Baiba at the airport. The holiday is extremely emotional for both of them. It takes several days before Wallander can unwind sufficiently to explain to Baiba exactly what he has been through. She understands, as her late husband was of course also a policeman. But when Wallander asks her to marry him she turns him down. She cannot think of remarrying yet as she is still far from over her loss. Wallander realises the time is not right and thinks that perhaps he should settle for continuing their relationship as it is. At least it has lifted him out of loneliness. As the book ends he is heading off on holiday to Italy with his father. Both men are excited by the trip. It is the first time his father has been in an aeroplane and Wallander is delighted to see his child-like enthusiasm.

On television the 500 pages of this enthralling story has to be massively simplified and cleverly edited into 90 minutes of screen time. There are many subtle changes but, remarkably, the essential elements are all still there. Kenneth Branagh's exceptional acting skill again enables him to convey the full range of powerful and diverse emotions that Kurt Wallander experiences. Somehow *Sidetracked* seems equally absorbing on TV as it is in literary form.

In fact some scenes, such as Wallander's reaction to the

girl's devastating death in the rapeseed, are even more moving on screen. The unshaven and unprepared TV version of Wallander is totally shattered by what he sees happen and Branagh makes our hero appear totally traumatised. His later scenes with Jeany Spark as Linda are particularly well written and played, given that they are getting across in a few glances and exchanges information and emotion which fills pages of text. She can tell from the look on his face that he has forgotten to buy his father a birthday present. Richard Cottan's script of course leans heavily on Mankell's novel but it has a real life and energy of its own. Even the bad guys get some good lines, like: 'Sweden stands for a little more than Bjorn Borg, Abba and a bit of skinny dipping in mountain lakes.'

Branagh handles Wallander's ambivalent attitude to the young criminal profiler superbly. After listening to a mind-numbing briefing, Wallander remarks dryly: 'Now we know we're looking for someone who seems completely normal.' When Ann-Britt appeals to Wallander to give the young man a chance he adds: 'He makes me feel about 108. Nice suit, though.'

Best of all, the intensity of the book is equalled and at times even surpassed as the investigation drives on to its shocking finale. *Sidetracked* is one of the very best *Wallander* stories and this production certainly does it justice.

Sidetracked was first published in Sweden in 1995 and appeared in an English translation in 1999. It won the Crime Writers' Gold Dagger in 2001 and it was the first of Mankell's *Wallander* stories to be issued in this country on audio cassette. Writer Sue Arnold praised the book perceptively in the *Guardian*: 'It took me a while to warm to Mankell's detective Kurt Wallander. He isn't a smug intellectual like Adam Dalgliesh or cosy like Reg Wexford, or drunk and disorderly like Rebus. Wallander is gloomily Scandinavian – sensitive, low-key and shockable – and believe me, there's much to be shocked at in this gripping drama about a serial killer who puts on war paint, axes his victims to death and then scalps them. The ones he really doesn't like fare much worse. This isn't a whodunit; we know the killer's identity. The fun is seeing how Wallander gets his man, assisted as always by those three time-honoured muses, hard work, happenstance and hunch. *Sidetracked* is the most exciting crime novel I've read for years, and the sooner we get some of Mankell's earlier ones the better.'

In the *Los Angeles Times* in 1999, Eugen Weber wrote: 'There's a fine new writer abroad, writing police whodunits, and the abroad is Sweden... Henning Mankell's writing is moreish, his style expansive, his details are sharply observed... Mankell's latest offering, *Sidetracked*, is about the unexpected murder of a former minister of justice, the fiery suicide of an unidentified young woman, more brutal and apparently unconnected killings and the skein of corruption, crime and cover-ups that ties them together. It exposes the narrow margin between sanity and lunacy. And it meshes social commentary with police work, now plodding around in circles, now spurting forward after accidental discovery or sudden illumination, always obeying the supreme injunction: "Only connect!"... *Sidetracked* again presents Mankell at his best; the evil hanky-panky continues, the slow, patient, harassed police work is tightly laid out. Strained, sleepless, overworked and driven, Wallander remains as solid and credible as ever. If you haven't read *Faceless Killers*, you have something to look forward to. If you haven't bought *Sidetracked*, do so ASAP.'

CHAPTER NINE:

THE FIFTH WOMAN

Kurt Wallander is in rare good spirits as *The Fifth Woman* opens. It is September 1994 and he has just returned from the trip to Rome with his father, which has gone surprisingly well. His father has suffered no apparent signs of his looming Alzheimer's disease that pushed Kurt to organise the holiday quickly and the two men have thoroughly enjoyed their time in the sunshine together. Mankell permits a hint of humour as Kurt watches his father staring at Michelangelo's ceiling in the Sistine Chapel for almost an hour and begins to wonder if he is searching for a grouse or a sunset in the huge fresco.

Ever the detective, Kurt asks the helpful English-speaking night desk worker to tip him off if his father ever goes out on his own, and he finds himself tailing his dad across the city through the night at one point. It seems the old boy is just making another sentimental journey, sitting contentedly on the Spanish Steps and taking in the magical scene just one more time. Wallander does not disturb his father and next day both men return from their holiday refreshed and tanned.

Back in Ystad all is deceptively peaceful. Wallander is just about to continue his long-running and deeply unproductive investigation into car smuggling from southern Sweden into former Eastern Bloc countries. He knows he can continue with that until he retires in 15 years time without any great chance of success. He gets on well with new Chief, Lisa Holgersson, until she asks him to give a lecture to eager new police recruits, which has him instantly running for cover. But a mystery burglary of a flower shop where nothing is stolen, followed by the discovery of two ingeniously cruel murders, soon kick-starts the action. A man is lured to fall into a deadly pit and impaled on sharpened bamboo stakes and left to die. Another is kidnapped just as he is about to fly off on holiday and later killed. No one misses him at first as he is supposed to be away for a fortnight. Wallander is soon immersed in a bewildering investigation with its roots in the savage killing of four nuns in Africa many years earlier.

Although Wallander's relationship with his father is still on a high, all is not so sunny with the women in the detective's life. Linda is working as a waitress to try to help fund her studies at a private theatre school in Stockholm. But she is not answering her telephone or returning any of her father's calls. He becomes frustrated. While in Rome he has reconsidered his proposal of marriage to Baiba Leipa. Although she had said, when they were on holiday together in Skagen, that she did not wish to be the wife of a policeman again, Wallander is still sure he wants her to be his wife and he decides to redouble his efforts to make it happen. He vows to move to a house with a garden to be able to offer more of a home for her, and even to get the dog he has been dreaming about for so long. Wallander telephones Baiba and repeats his proposal. Baiba says she still has doubts about getting married again but agrees to come over for a holiday to talk about it. Wallander is pleased and it distracts him from the latest irritating police initiative known as 'local police', which he is certain will distract efforts from important matters like solving crimes.

An excellent example of Mankell's ability to bring the reader at times uncomfortably close to Kurt Wallander arrives when the detective is woken in the middle of the night suffering from a stomach upset and severe diarrhoea. He's not sure whether to blame a late night pizza or a bug but in any case he phones in sick to the police station. 'All I know is that I'm puking and shitting,' says Wallander to Martinsson, who surely must feel this is more information than he needs about the condition of his boss's digestive system. It's hard to think of any other fictional crime-fighter uttering a line like that but somehow, coming from Wallander, it is anything but unexpected. It is as if every aspect of his life is to be served up for the readers.

Mankell expertly sets his stories against a backdrop of real events. Before the investigation into the savage murders really gets under way, the whole police station is saddened by the news of a terrible ferry disaster. The *MS Estonia* was on its way across the Baltic from Tallinn to Stockholm when it sank on 28 September 1994. Some 852 people lost their lives in what was one of the worst maritime disasters of the late twentieth century. A number of Swedish police officers died in the disaster so the sinking has a special resonance with Wallander and his colleagues, and the way the tragedy is woven into this fictional story adds massively to the credibility of the adventure.

Wallander soon gets his mind back onto the murder inquiry. The savagery of impaling a man on bamboo stakes and leaving him to slowly die shocks him to the core. 'It could be an act of blind hatred or insanity, but cold calculation lay behind the murder,' thinks Wallander. He can't decide which scares him more. The crime really gives him food for thought and soon afterwards another body is found, tied to a tree in a forest. It is clearly another killing that has been meticulously planned and callously carried out. Wallander realises they are dealing with a formidable and determined murderer and they still don't have the remotest idea of a motive, or if the two killings are definitely linked. Wallander reflects how quickly his happiness over the successful holiday with his father, his decision to buy a house and Baiba's impending visit is replaced by depression over this shocking investigation. He finds his world crumbling away beneath his feet and he wonders how long he can keep on being a policeman.

Somehow Wallander finds time to visit his father and enjoys looking at his photographs of their trip to Rome.

Wallander asks his father how many times he has painted the same landscape scene and the old man has no idea and wonders why his son always asks the same question. Wallander long ago assumed that the reason his father kept repeating the same scene was because of some deep-seated desire to keep at bay all of the many things that were changing around him. The two men take a walk along the nearby beach together. Wallander's father comments on the beauty of the scene and Kurt realises that the Rome trip has brought him some deep satisfaction. It has been the journey of a lifetime. Wallander's father seems much less troubled and more at peace with himself though does admit to 'feeling bad'. They walk for more than two hours before Wallander's father decides they have had enough. Wallander has to rush back to Ystad to the police station for a meeting but is glad they have spent the time together. He thinks at last he and his father are growing close again and hopes that he can regain the warmer relationship they had before he upset his father by deciding to join the police force. Wallander wonders thoughtfully to himself if he will ever know why his father could never accept him becoming a policeman.

Just when he is least expecting it, the terrible news arrives in a phone call. Wallander is leaving his office after another exhausting day when he hears it ring. For a second he hesitates, then typically turns back to answer it. It is Gertrud in floods of tears. She says: 'You have to come right away... your father is dead. He's lying in his studio in the middle of his paintings.' Wallander leaves the police station without speaking to anyone and drives fast to Löderup. He is convinced that Gertrud is mistaken and that his father has simply passed out. He rushes into his father's studio and sees for himself that Gertrud is not mistaken. His father is dead and his body is lying across the painting he had been working on. He had shut his eyes tight but his hand is still clutching the paintbrush he used to add the tiny dabs of white to the grouse's feathers. Wallander realises his father was just finishing the painting he had been working on the day before, when they had walked along the beach together so contentedly. Wallander is stunned. He shakes his father, as if to try to put life back into him. He knows well enough from his job that death always arrives at the wrong time and when it comes it disrupts everything.

Gertrud is distraught and Wallander tries to comfort her without understanding his own feelings. He feels completely empty inside and realises that he does not honestly feel anything at all apart from a vague unease that it is unfair that his father has been taken from him now, when at last they were beginning to get on well together. But he also realises that he cannot feel sorry for his father. When the ambulance arrives Wallander finds he knows the driver, who tries to comfort him by saying that it was probably a stroke, which would have been a very quick end. Later a doctor confirms this diagnosis and adds that a blood vessel had burst in his father's brain and he would have had no idea that he was dying. Gertrud is devastated by her husband's sudden death but her grief is spliced with relief that he did not suffer a long and painful illness full of angry confusion as a result of his Alzheimer's. But Wallander is angry that his father was alone when he died and, although he was 80, he feels that it is still much too early to go. He was not ready to say goodbye to his father. After the ambulance has taken away his father's body, with Gertrud in tearful accompaniment, Wallander stands alone in the studio surrounded by the familiar smell of turpentine and weeps uncontrollably at the thought of his father leaving his final grouse uncompleted. Mankell cleverly provides an enthralling view of his hero's next actions when he writes: 'As a gesture towards the invisible border between life and death, Wallander took the paintbrush and filled in the two white points that were still missing from the grouse's plumage. It was the first time in his life that he had touched any of his father's paintings with a brush.' Wallander then cleans the brush and replaces it with the others in the old jam jar his father always used.

He rings Ebba at the station and she is upset and very sad. Wallander is so choked he can scarcely speak but manages to explain that he will not be coming back to work. He does compose himself long enough to insist that he still wants to be kept in touch with any developments in the investigation. Next he calls his sister Kristina to break the bad news and then he rings Mona at work, at a beauty shop in Malmö. Mona thinks at first something must have happened to Linda and seems faintly relieved when he says his father has died. Wallander is angry but manages not to say anything. Mona becomes more sympathetic and says she knows what he is going through as he has been afraid of this moment all his life. Wallander rings Baiba in Riga but there is no answer. He goes back into the studio and sits worrying about his own mortality until Linda finally rings back. She and her father find they are both crying over the phone to each other. She promises to come over as soon as she can.

That evening Wallander, Gertrud and Linda discuss the funeral arrangements. Wallander doubts that his father would have wanted a church service but Gertrud wants to have a vicar so he goes along with it. Kristina arrives and points out to her brother that now their father is dead, they are next in line. Wallander is already feeling miserable enough and he can feel his fear of his own death growing all the time. But he doesn't talk about it to anyone. Eventually, Wallander manages to talk to Baiba on the telephone and she is enormously comforting. She talks about how she felt when her own father died ten years earlier and also about how she was affected by the death of her husband Karlis, which led to her meeting with Wallander. Afterwards Wallander is enormously relieved to think that Baiba is still very much a part of his life. He is further heartened by a phone call from his old friend, Sten Widen. Wallander is not sure Sten had ever met his father but he is still grateful for the call. Mona comes over to visit for supper and tries to take Kurt's and Linda's minds off the death of the old man. It works to an extent, as Wallander at last accepts after talking to his ex-wife that his marriage is finally over. It takes the death of his father to make him realise that that chapter of his life is finished. But although his emotions are still churning and his grief is harder to deal with than he had imagined, Wallander still has to control a complex murder investigation. Chief Holgersson does suggest he might like to take some time off but he refuses, insisting that his grief eases when he is working.

The funeral is not quite the ordeal that he had been dreading, partly thanks to the fact that it is conducted by an attractive woman vicar he has already met. He is relieved when it is all over but he wonders how he will manage without his father in his life to worry about. He feels his own generation is particularly unprepared to accept that death can always be round the corner, and this is true of him too even though he has to deal with death at work so much. Linda shows her emotions during the service more openly than anyone else. Wallander knows that she had really loved her grandfather and he worries that he will not see as much of her now that he has gone. But Linda promises she will visit him more often in future and Wallander says he will not forget Gertrud. Wallander is left with one nagging regret now his father is gone; he will never know why his father objected so strongly to him joining the police force. It has puzzled him for years and now it is a riddle to which he will never know the answer.

Wallander and his team pull out all the stops to find a link between the two dead men. On the surface they are completely different and there does not appear to be a connection. The man who was impaled on bamboo poles in a pit on his own land was a car dealer who lived quietly alone and wrote poetry. The other guy was a florist who was kidnapped and starved for days before being left for dead, tied to a tree half-naked in the woods. Both killings display a disturbing level of cruelty but there doesn't seem to be a link. Wallander is puzzled when Linda starts showing an interest in the investigation but then she stuns him with a question. 'Do you think I would make a good policewoman?' she asks her father. He says she might but they do not discuss it further and he does not dwell on the sudden query. He is too enveloped in his enquiries into the two murders. The heartless manner of both killings really gets to him. Death can be depressing and Wallander reflects that it has not been easy seeing the corpse of his father lying there among all his paintings. He desperately wants to see Baiba. The nagging loneliness and the deaths in his life are really getting him down. He realises that he has been divorced for five years and he is on his way to becoming 'an old shaggy dog' who is scared of people and commitment. He thinks to himself that that is something he definitely does not want to be.

In order to keep his promise to Linda, Kurt telephones Gertrud and is happy to hear her sounding cheerful. Her sister has come over to stay and help her go through his father's possessions. The old man had always lived very simply and there are almost no debts. The estate consists mainly of the house in Löderup. Gertrud asked Wallander if there is anything of his father's he would like to have. Wallander says no, but then thinks again and asks if he can have one of his father's landscapes, one with a grouse but not the one he was working on when he died.

Forcing himself to re-examine the facts of the case that they have so far, Wallander detects a possible link between one of the men and mercenary action in Africa in the 1960s. He goes to interview a former Swedish United Nations official about the world of the mercenary and realises some past event may be connected to the two terrible murders. The police hold a press conference to try to get the sort of coverage that might help the investigation, and Wallander finds himself answering questions from reporters inquiring about plans by some of the residents of Lodinge, unhappy about the police's ability to protect them, to start a citizen militia. Wallander is taken aback and writes such moves off as 'collective stupidity'. But the reporter presses on and says the residents are reacting to the brutal murders and believe the Swedish police have given in to criminal elements and so need to organise their own security. Publicly, Wallander speaks out angrily and insists such a militia would be illegal and anyone taking part will be prosecuted. But privately he is more than a little sympathetic to the residents of Lodinge or any group of frightened people in modern Sweden. Wallander understands that people feel the Sweden of late-1994 is not as solid or as stable as they thought it was. The high-rise buildings are widely described as 'inhuman' and Wallander feels it is inevitable that some of the people forced to live in them will struggle to keep their 'humanity'. He sees native Swedes who feel unwanted or unwelcome in their own country and react with violence. Wallander feels deeply about the plight of his country and he hates the way that society has grown cruel. He often questions himself about how it is possible to sustain a police career and he sees many of his colleagues seriously considering changing to alternative, less stressful jobs.

Wallander delves deep into the private life of the first murder victim and discovers he was a brutal sadist who abused his wife into an early grave. Wallander is convinced the man's son knows more about his father and questions him closely. But the son surprises Wallander with a direct question about domestic violence when he asks him: 'Did you ever hit your wife?' Wallander is taken aback and parries the inquiry with another question. But his mind goes back to the time he lost his temper and hit Mona. She fell back and hit her head on the door post and blacked out for a few seconds. He goes cold with guilt as he recalls the incident. Mona had almost packed her bags and left him then. He knows that the only reason she didn't was because Linda was so young. He had grovelled and apologised and begged her to stay and in the end she did. He didn't understand where his outburst of rage had come from. Today he can't even remember what they were arguing about but he can't think of any act in his life that he is more ashamed of.

As his investigations take him away from Ystad, Wallander manages to find time to meet his daughter Linda. It turns into a real heart-to-heart which reveals much about both father and daughter. Wallander confesses to Linda that he was jealous of how close she was to his father and tells Linda how he had always wondered why his father could never accept his decision to become a policeman. Linda tries to explain that her grandfather was pretty eccentric and then changes the subject and asks her father again what he would think if she decided to become a policewoman. Wallander is not sure what to think or say. He asks Linda about her acting lessons but she doesn't want to talk about them at all. Wallander is concerned about how swiftly his daughter changes her mind about her career. He thinks she makes too many rash decisions. Linda suddenly asks her father why it is 'so difficult to live' in Sweden. It is a sweeping question full of levels of meaning but Wallander answers very simply: 'Sometimes I think it's because we have stopped darning our socks.'

Linda is bewildered but Wallander is serious. He explains that when he was a boy growing up Sweden was still a country where people darned the holes in their socks. He even learned to do it at school for himself. But all of a sudden one day, the idea of darning a sock was desperately old fashioned and the most outdated idea on earth. Any socks which developed holes were instantly thrown out and replaced by new ones. It was the beginning of the throw away society and it wasn't just socks. Mankell has Wallander articulate the massive increase in materialism through the example of ever replaceable socks. But he has the detective extend it so that, as well as their socks, people were throwing away their principles and their moral code. The old ways of politeness and consideration for others were replaced by a sort of surly competitiveness that increased the amount of aggression and violence in everyday life enormously.

Each generation grows further away from the old ways of solidarity, with the strongest and richest helping those less fortunate than themselves. Wallander is a little woolly and vague and he wonders aloud to Linda that perhaps he is not getting his point across clearly enough. But Linda insists she knows what he is trying to say. He considers that every generation probably thinks younger people don't conduct their lives as well as they did. Linda points out that her grandfather never said anything critical about younger people and the way they live.

Wallander insists that his father lived in his own closed world, shutting himself away and painting his pictures. He snorts that in his father's pictures and in his life, everything stayed the same and nothing changed. He says his father put up an invisible wall around his studio and himself. Linda speaks up for her dead grandfather and says he knew a lot about life and that he wrote some lovely poems. Wallander has not got the remotest idea that his father wrote poems and says so. Linda says her grandfather showed her some of his poetry and she adds that she writes poems as well. Wallander accepts that he could never write poetry himself. He lives in an ugly world full of bureaucracy, police reports and forensic records – hardly poetic. Linda swiftly changes the subject and asks her father how his relationship is developing with Baiba. He reveals that most of all he would like her to come to Ystad and live with him. Linda shakes her head and her father wants to know why. 'Don't be offended,' she says. 'But I hope you realise you're a difficult person to live with.'

Wallander is taken aback. He can't understand this deeply personal criticism from his daughter and asks why she says such a thing. Linda smiles patiently and tells her father to think about her mother and ask himself why she wanted to move out and live a different life. Wallander feels he is being judged unfairly and looks annoyed. Linda realises her father is angered by a remark that has struck home hard. He insists he is not angry, simply tired. Linda moves next to her father and tells him she loves him but points out she is an adult and their conversations are going to be more grown-up in future. Father and daughter then settle down to watch a film on television and Wallander understands that this is how their future relationship will be, more open and honest. As he lies in bed later, he tells himself he must accept that his little girl has grown up but he can't decide whether this makes him a winner or a loser. Next morning as he sees Linda off on her train, she bursts into tears. He is baffled but she says she misses her grandfather and she dreams about him every night. Wallander hugs his daughter but after the train pulls away he is left alone on the platform feeling completely desolate. The intrepid investigator does not know how he can carry on but work soon galvanises him back into action.

A new lead sends Wallander to interview a very dangerous man. He breaks all police rules as he confronts this muscle-bound and aggressive man alone, threatening him with arrest to persuade him to talk. But it seems to be a dead end and Wallander rushes off instead to take a look at the missing suitcase of the man who was murdered before he could take his trip. On the surface, the contents appear to provide no clues but a hint of perfume, and Wallander's remarkable insight that the case was packed by a woman, gives the detectives the clear indication that their murderer might well not be a man. The other members of the team are astonished that Wallander knows that men and women are inclined to pack a suitcase in two very different ways. It is a great Mankell example of the wisdom of Wallander, unspectacular but enormously important to the investigation. Just as the team make what feels like a breakthrough, the deadly woman avenger is claiming her next victim. A man is grabbed from the street, drugged and then trussed up inside a bag full of weights and deposited into a lake. It is another shocking sequence.

Still ignorant of this further slaying, Wallander realises he needs a woman's insight and he leans heavily on young Ann-Britt Höglund. With her husband away, she is having babysitter problems and invites Wallander back to her flat to continue their brainstorming of the existing evidence. Ann-Britt is reluctant to believe that a woman could be responsible for such horrific crimes but after she has considered the case she accepts it could be possible. They talk it over until the early hours of the morning until Wallander realises his colleague is exhausted. Her husband is away and Wallander sympathises with her position of holding down such an important, all-consuming job while caring for her children. He tells Ann-Britt that for the first time he sees how hard it is for her and admits that when Linda was little, he always had Mona to look after her. He cannot recall a single time when domestic pressures forced him home from a demanding investigation. Wallander borrows Ann-Britt's car to drive home and as he leaves he tell her she is 'a very good police officer'. This is high praise from Wallander and he can see that she is very pleased.

Next day at the police station, in a rare quiet moment, Wallander reaches out for the telephone to ring his father. A second later he realises that is impossible and grief hits him like a cold shower. He has no father to ring any more and he never will have. A wave of depression sweeps over him and he dials the number anyway and Gertrud answers almost straight away. He asks how she is and she bursts into tears. Wallander finds himself very moved as well. Gertrud says she is just trying to take one day at a time and Wallander promises to drive down to see her that afternoon. Gertrud is grateful and says there is still so much about his father that she does not know. Wallander reveals that he feels the same and suggests that they may be able to fill in some of the gaps in each other's knowledge. But after he hangs up, Wallander regrets his offer to drive to Löderup as he knows how much work he has. There is an important sequence of introspection. Wallander feels frustrated and angry that so often he disappoints those he loves. He furiously breaks a pen he is holding and hurls it into the wastepaper basket. He suddenly feels like running out of the police station and far away from his desperately demanding job. He asks himself when he last talked to Baiba and why hadn't she called him? Is their relationship withering due to the distance involved and the lack of sufficient emotion between them?

When is he going to do something about his long held ambition to move to a house and buy a dog? He knows that sometimes he really hates his job and wishes that he could escape from it for good. He thinks about the prosecutor, Per Akeson, who intends to exchange the grind of legal work in Ystad for a more interesting job with the United Nations in Africa. He recalls a conversation he had with Baiba in which she'd said everyone in the West seemed to have the same fantasy that one day they could all get on board an enormous yacht and sail away to the sunshine of the Caribbean. Pulling down the Berlin Wall and the collapse of the Eastern bloc had opened many people's eyes in her country, Latvia, but she sees that there is poverty in apparently rich countries like Sweden as well. The feeling of unhappiness and dissatisfaction is everywhere, Wallander concludes. That is why everyone dreams of escape to the sunshine.

Mankell cleverly weaves more developments of the 'citizen militia' enthusiasts into the compelling narrative. As the police struggle to solve the mystery of the murders, the alarming publicity grows and so do the ambitions of the people who want to form defence groups. Reports in the local paper record that protective groups are springing up in several towns in Skåne. Chief Holgersson says gloomily: 'We're going to end up with vigilante groups all over the country. Imagine a situation where pseudo policemen outnumber us.' The feeling of a whole society finding itself embattled and undermined is constantly reinforced. The discovery of the body in a sack in a lake does nothing to lift police spirits. Wallander realises instantly that their killer has struck again but, frustratingly, he is no closer to arresting him or, more probably, her. When they reach the scene Wallander finds that the sack has a hole in it. He knows what this means. The man was alive when he was put into the lake and frantically tried to kick his way out as he drowned.

Wallander feels sick but he presses on and soon finds himself interviewing the man's widow, along with an officer called Birch from the nearby force in Lund. He has worked with Birch before and they are roughly the same age and with similar disenchantment about the state of the country and the changing role of the police in an ever more violent society. Birch remembers an old commissioner who used to warn young detectives that savage crimes would become more widespread because Sweden's prosperity was a 'well-camouflaged quagmire'. There was decay underneath the glittering surface that would one day emerge to envelop them all. Birch says that when his old boss used to say this, he did not understand what he meant but now he fully comprehends and fears that he was absolutely right. The two officers are surprised as they break the news to the widow that her husband is dead. She shows no emotion and when they ask if she knows of anyone who might have wanted to kill her husband, she says herself. Birch and Wallander are astonished and even more shocked when, after they ask what he has done to make her feel this way, she rips off her blouse and shows them injuries on her body. The woman has been clearly cruelly abused by her vicious husband so she is hardly likely to be upset at news of his death. It's another impressive example of Mankell's mastery of cleverly combining social comment with stirring narrative.

As the hunt for the murderous woman intensifies, Wallander finds himself pacing up and down in a hospital car park late at night waiting for Svedberg to elicit some vital information. Suddenly, in his mind Wallander is back in Rome, on the trail of his father who was undertaking his secret midnight mission towards the Spanish Steps. Wallander looks back thoughtfully on his father and that trip. An old man in an ancient city... did he know that he did not have long to live? Wallander begins to feel emotional and wonders when, if ever, he will have the chance to deal with the grief that he still feels for his father. And then he considers his own position yet again. He will soon be 50 and what he fears most is that the world will become so unfriendly and strange that he will no longer be able to handle it. He fears being shunted away from the front line of crime-fighting to see out his years until retirement doing a dull desk job or visiting schools or village halls and giving lectures on safe driving or the dangers of drugs. To Wallander, that would be half a life. He still wants his house in the country, his dog and Baiba. Not for the first time, he resolves that he must take firm and positive action to make these changes in his life sooner rather than later. But he is quickly distracted when a man is found badly injured at the side of a road. He has a note which has been stapled to his skin saying: 'A burglar neutralised by the night guards.'

Wallander is staggered and permits himself a rare use of the foulest language to convey his feelings. It turns out that the man lost his way late at night and stopped to ask for directions. The people he asked were part of a new 'citizen's militia' who immediately decided that if he was out and about at this time, he must be up to no good and so beat the living daylights out of him. Wallander is furious and insists on going out to arrest as many members of the so-called militia as he can find. Hansson goes with him but thinks they are massively overreacting. Wallander says they are going to catch some dangerous people. He says that he cannot think of a group who posed more of a threat to the rule of law in Sweden than these people trying to take the law into their own hands and badly injuring an innocent person. They arrive as visibly as possible, with sirens blaring, and arrest the leader. Wallander has asked Ebba to tip off the press so a photographer catches an image of the man being handcuffed and led away. The man's wife suddenly races out of the house and attacks Hansson, giving the photographer more excellent action pictures. Wallander pauses to tell the press that they are acting because a number of individuals attacked and battered an innocent man last night. The attackers appear to be part of some kind of citizen's militia. They claim the man was a burglar and beat him almost to death. Wallander manages to persuade the 'leader' to come clean and give them the names of other vigilante members.

Wallander wastes no time holding a press conference and explains in detail to reporters what has happened. A perfectly innocent man asks for directions late at night and is instantly presumed to be a burglar and beaten very badly by an organised gang. He uses this example of people-power getting completely out of control to ram home his message that it is up to the police to protect the community. It is a job which needs to be done professionally and in a properly organised manner. Wallander says he hopes people will be dissuaded from joining in such illegal activity by this incident. Fortunately, the victim is likely to make a full recovery but he has been savagely attacked and might very well have lost his life. He hopes that the vigilantes who had now owned up to carrying out the assault would receive sentences that serve as a deterrent to other people considering getting together and taking the law into their own hands. Afterwards, Chief Holgersson compliments Wallander and tells him he handled the press conference really well. Ann-Britt and Hansson applaud when he walks over to them but he is not amused. He needs to get out of the police station and clear his head; dealing with the press was never easy and he needs to calm down and re-focus on the inquiry into the murders. He wonders why he cannot seem to combine a happy home life with his job as a policeman. He notes that Martinsson has an excellent relationship with his family and Ann-Britt seems to cope well despite having almost total responsibility for her two children as her husband is away so much. Wallander goes to the bathroom and washes his face after a long meeting about the murder hunt. He looks at himself in the mirror and becomes convinced that his appearance has changed since the death of his father. He knows he must make time to seriously consider how he feels about the impact of the death of his father. He also knows he must do something definite about his relationship with Baiba, the woman he loves but never seems able to find the time to telephone.

For Wallander the job is everything. Mankell shows how his hero yearns for a woman to love and cherish and a happy home life, but he is clearly never able to detach himself from his job long enough to do anything about it. He eventually does phone Baiba but he detects a certain wariness in her voice with regard to himself. He asks why she doesn't come over and she retorts that he never rings her and, even when he does, he often has to cut their conversation short to rush off back to his work. So many home truths are difficult to deal with for a proud policeman. Wallander becomes angry and slams down the phone with great force. Very quickly he regrets doing it but he knows Baiba well enough to know that if he rings back now she will not take the call. He can't understand the strength of his fury that forced him to slam down the phone and he wonders grimly what would have happened if they had held the same conversation face to face. He instantly switches back into work mode. He has been through a seven-hour meeting with his investigation team and he is exhausted, yet he still has the drive to register he must ask one more question that will nudge him that bit closer to making an arrest. Next morning he rings Baiba and says that he is exhausted. Baiba accepts that but she still wants to know if he really wants her to come over to Sweden to see him. He insists he does and she says she will try to plan a trip for a few weeks time. Wallander is briefly elated. This time he will have a serious go at getting her to come and live with him in a new house in the country, with a dog for company.

At the police station next morning there is another shock. Martinsson's young schoolgirl daughter has been attacked by older pupils, simply because her father is a police officer. Worse still, it seems to Wallander that the publicity against the vigilantes is being turned on its head, with stories that the man they apprehended fought back and that they are really innocent. Wallander is furious about the way the newspapers are covering the events but powerless to do anything about it. It seems that other pupils stood around laughing while the girl was attacked by boys. Wallander goes to Martinsson's home where the officer is comforting his distraught daughter. Martinsson says that he is quitting the police force. He says that the job is not worth it when it starts to affect your family. Wallander can do nothing but agree with that sentiment. He desperately does not want Martinsson to quit because he is a very good officer but he can understand that his family must come first. Martinsson's wife is also very upset and she asks Wallander: 'All this violence? Where does it come from?' He answers that it is because the country is changing, not because there are more evil people. She says bleakly that Sweden has become so cold-hearted and Wallander can do nothing but agree. All the police officers are upset and angry over the attack and see themselves even more under siege, trying to fight to hold the peace lines in a nation that seems to want to go to war with itself. Wallander knows that he must try to dissuade Martinsson from leaving the police. He is a good officer that they cannot afford to lose. But he knows that if Martinsson decides to put his family first after this shocking assault then there is nothing that he can do. Wallander keeps in touch with Martinsson over the new few days, taking every chance to keep him in touch with the investigation. He does not want to lose a good officer if he can help it and he holds back from trying to talk him out of his decision to quit, although he manages to convince him to delay writing his letter of resignation for a day or so.

Whenever he is struggling to move the investigation forward Wallander turns to Ann-Britt Höglund for advice. Her quick mind makes her the most responsive and helpful of his colleagues. He calls Ann-Britt and says they have too many holes in their information. He explains: 'We have to make the gaps speak and the pieces we do have tell us about things that have hidden meanings. We have to try to see through the events, turn them on their heads in order to set them on their feet.' Ann-Britt is very impressed. She says that no one ever spoke like that at the police academy and she asks Wallander if he was ever invited to give a lecture there. Wallander says that he can't give lectures but Ann-Britt persists and tells her boss that is exactly what he can do. Later, Wallander wonders if Ann-Britt is right. He has always rejected the idea of passing on his experience to young officers in such a formal way but he starts to wonder if that might be a genuine career choice for the future. When Wallander sits down with Martinsson to consider the younger man's future with the police force, he is not surprised to see Martinsson looking very dejected. Martinsson is desperately unsure what to do and asks Wallander for advice. He says his wife and daughter have both advised him not to leave but he feels he does not want to put his family in danger in any way. Wallander tells Martinsson about his own feelings after shooting the man in the fog and killing him. He took a year off work and seriously considered quitting the job altogether. Instead he took his time to get over the incident and eventually returned to work. Wallander tells Martinsson that he knows now it was the right decision for him. He advises Martinsson that, of course, the decision is up to him but he should not do anything rash and should take time to make up his mind. Wallander assures Martinsson that he is a good policeman and everyone notices when he is not there. He is irreplaceable. Martinsson is very moved by this support from a boss he deeply respects. He thinks about it for a few moments and then he goes out of the room, gets his jacket and suggests they get back to work.

The climax of *The Fifth Woman* is one of Mankell's masterpieces. I don't want to spoil anyone's surprise when they read it for the first time but it does include a moment when Wallander fears he has put Ann-Britt's life in great danger. Extraordinarily, he seriously considers shooting himself dead, at least for a second or two. Ann-Britt appears in the following books so it is clear she survives but Wallander is still furious with himself for what he knows could have been a fatal mistake. The incident has a traumatic effect on him. He waits in the hospital for hours until he is told Ann-Britt's condition has stabilised. Then he drives to his father's graveside and stands there feeling completely wrecked by his experiences. Eventually he goes home and phones Baiba. She seems to understand what he is going through and they talk for a long time. At three o'clock in the morning he returns to the hospital and sits unmoving and silently waiting. At one point he bursts into uncontrollable tears and locks himself in the bathroom. But then he returns to his chair. The doctor at last comes up with the news that Wallander has been praying for. Ann-Britt is out of danger and likely to make a full recovery from her injuries. Afterwards, Wallander visits Ann-Britt in hospital every day. Other officers try to reassure him that he is not to blame but he is not convinced.

Wallander's greatest support during this time is his daughter, Linda. She comes back to Ystad and does her best to take care of him. She talks endlessly about what had happened and slowly manages to make her father at least consider the possibility that Ann-Britt's shooting was not his complete responsibility. In the conclusion to this captivating novel, Mankell gently makes the point that there is a link between the 'citizen's militia' who want to take the law into their own hands and the murderer who has her own terrible reasons for wanting revenge.

Wallander takes a long time to get over his anguish over the shooting of Ann-Britt. He slowly recovers a little of his confidence and goes ahead with his plans to move house, bring Baiba over to become his wife and get a dog. He looks at a possible house where he thinks they could settle. He convinces Baiba to come over for a trip to Skagen with him and Linda that he hopes will end happily. And he goes to a kennels to be introduced to some adorable black Labradors. It's about as close as Henning Mankell and Kurt Wallander ever come to a happy ending.

The Fifth Woman was first published in Sweden in 1996 but was not published in Britain in translation until 2003. Praise for *The Fifth Woman* came from all over the world. A review in the French newspaper *Le Monde* said: 'Inspector Wallander is one of the most wonderful creations in contemporary crime writing... a classic of its genre.'

Peter Gutteridge wrote in the *Observer*: 'The eponymous fifth woman is in the company of four nuns in Africa when they are all killed in a savage night-time attack. Later that year, back in Sweden, a series of revenge killings begins. Wallander and his close-knit team use solid police procedure rather than intuition or imaginative flights to solve the crime. It confirms that Mankell is one of the most ingenious crime writers around, strong on characterisation, plotting and atmosphere. Highly recommended.'

CHAPTER TEN:
ONE STEP BEHIND

Curious killings are one of the many memorable features of Mankell's *Wallander* novels, and *One Step Behind* opens with one of the very strangest. Three young people meet in a remote wood on Midsummer's Eve to act out an elaborate masque. They have costumes recalling the days of the 18th century, including corsets, cravats and ruffles. They also have music, food and drink, and a carefully rehearsed plan to have fun. But an uninvited fourth person with a gun arrives and shoots all three dead. It is a shocking, shattering start and once this book has begun, the pace never falters. The killing is ingeniously covered up and the young people are thought to have left Sweden for a while to go travelling. The relatives of the dead youngsters react in a very relaxed way when they stop hearing from them, apart from one mother who is convinced that something terrible has happened to her daughter.

Meanwhile, all the high hopes for the brave new world Wallander was going to create for himself and his Latvian lover, Baiba, have already sadly been abandoned before the book begins. She came over to Ystad in December 1994, shortly after the death of Wallander's father and the dramatic events described in *The Fifth Woman*. Baiba and Linda got on very well and they spent a happy Christmas with Wallander. Just before Baiba was due to return to Riga, she and Kurt talked seriously about getting married and settling down together in Sweden. They looked at a house, which was part of an old farm outside Svenstorp, and everything seemed set fair for a happy future. But a few months after Baiba had gone back home, she rang to say she was having doubts. She had changed her mind and was not yet ready to get married and move to Sweden. Wallander tried to change her mind but the conversation turned awkward and ended in a row. He did fly over to Riga in the summer and they had long walks along the beach, with Baiba saying she wanted things to stay just as they were for a while. Wallander was unhappy and although Baiba visited him in Ystad again, the sound of wedding bells was definitely not on her schedule. She told Wallander she did not want to lose her job at the university. There would be no job for her in Sweden and she wanted to stay in her own country. She wanted them to leave things as they were. Baiba returned to Latvia and gradually the phone calls dried up. Wallander admitted later to Linda that it was all over.

It is now almost two years since Wallander's father

died but every time he drives to Löderup, he finds it hard to accept that his father will not be sitting there in his studio, paintbrush in hand, hard at work on the latest of his identical landscapes. Wallander's own health is not good. He feels very tired much of the time and even when he went on holiday with Linda, he found himself feeling listless and lacking in energy. He knows something is not right with his body so he makes an appointment to do something he hates – see the doctor. He and Gertrud have sorted out his father's things. She still lives in the house and a year went by before the cleared out his studio. They found 32 finished paintings, which they gave mostly to friends and family until they had just five left. But Gertrud has now decided she no longer wants to live in the house full of memories. She intends to move to live with her sister and the house is to be put up for sale. Wallander is on his way to meet the estate agent when he almost loses his life. He is feeling dozy as he drives along and the car drifts on to the opposite side of the road. Only a blast on the horn from a truck driver alerts Wallander to the danger and he swerves out of danger.

With his nerves still jangling, Wallander arrives at the house to sort out the last few of his father's belongings with Gertrud. He is dressed very casually and he is embarrassed when he sees Gertrud is wearing the outfit she had for her wedding to his father. This is an important day for Gertrud, her last day in the home she shared with great happiness with his father. The estate agent is Robert Åkerblom, the man whose wife was callously shot dead by Russian ex-KGB man

Konovalenko in *The Man Who Smiled*. Wallander recalls how the poor man burst into tears at the news of his wife's death and he attempts to sympathise. But Åkerblom explains that he has changed his life to work less and be able to spend more time with his daughters, and so the awkward moment passes. The price for the house is set and Wallander returns home to Ystad and rings his doctor for an appointment.

Wallander is feeling desperately lonely as *One Step Behind* begins. Apart from his daughter, he has almost no friends other than colleagues at work. Ann-Britt telephones to find out about how the arrangements for selling his father's house went and he reflects on how kind she is; he would never have thought of making such a call. He had dreamed of a new life with Baiba in a new house with a dog. But it has all come to nothing. Baiba is history and he does not want to move into a new house on his own, nor own a dog. He realises all he has is his job and all he has seen recently in the police is his workload increase enormously, while criminals appear to be enjoying more and more success. Crime might not have paid once in old-fashioned, law-abiding Sweden but times are changing and not for the better, thinks Wallander.

When he finally attends his doctor's appointment the diagnosis is very quick and instantly devastating. Wallander has a very high blood sugar level and has diabetes. The doctor tells him it is something that can be controlled but Wallander is still shocked. He tries to throw himself into his work and interviews a woman who is convinced her daughter has gone missing, despite receiving a postcard from her from Vienna saying she is enjoying her trip. The woman becomes hysterical in Wallander's office. She is convinced the postcard is a forgery and that something dreadful has happened to her daughter. After work Wallander attempts to start a new healthy eating regime. He also resolves to walk to work instead of driving and to take long walks along the beach at weekends. He even decides to see if Hansson is still interested in a game of badminton. He is determined not to be beaten by his diabetes, but when Linda calls to see how he is, he lies that the doctor did not find anything wrong with him. She sounds surprised at that and Wallander realises that his daughter sees right through him. He can't understand why he doesn't tell her the truth about his diabetes. It is not as if it is something to be ashamed of.

Self doubts and awkward personal questioning appear to be part and parcel of life in the Swedish police force. Ann-Britt is now back at work and apparently recovered from the gunshot wound she received in *The Fifth Woman*. But her optimism and self-confidence appear to have taken a major hit as she asks Wallander how he has lasted so long in this morale-draining job. She confides in Wallander that she and her husband are going through a difficult time and are considering a separation. She also finds herself unsure about her future in the police force. She is upset by reports of corrupt officers and seriously wonders how she is going to last another 30 years in the job. Wallander agrees that corruption in the justice system is worse than ever before but insists that is why it is more important that officers like herself stay in the force. Wallander says that he sticks in there by persuading himself that the police would be worse off without him. Ann-Britt is not convinced. She wonders what is happening to their country. Wallander has no answer and he talks about a tragic case of two 14-year-old boys attacking a 12-year-old. They didn't just beat up their victim but stomped on his head until he was dead. Wallander remembers a time when fights stopped if your opponent went to the floor. But the principle of 'You don't hit a man when he's down' has long gone. 'It's as if not caring has become the norm,' says Wallander sadly.

Mankell has many sublime skills as a thriller writer but perhaps one of the most distinctive is his ability to spring the sort of surprises that turn a simple page-turner into the sort of experience that can really shock and move the reader. I almost dropped my copy of *One Step Behind* when I discovered, along with Wallander and Martinsson, that Svedberg had been shot dead. The dogged, faithful, home-loving detective had been mysteriously missing for a few days before Wallander went in search of him. The sequence when Svedberg's body is discovered in his Ystad flat is simply unforgettable. Mankell writes that as Wallander gazes at the dead body of his friend and colleague: 'There was no doubt in his mind about what he was seeing. The man he had worked with for so many years was dead. He no longer existed. He would never again sit in his usual place at the table in one of the conference rooms, scratching his bald spot with the end of a pencil. Svedberg didn't have a bald spot any more. Half of his head was blown away.'

Most readers must have been blown away by this electrifying piece of writing. Svedberg has become like a friend to many of us over previous books. Wallander and Martinsson have no time to grieve. They go instantly into action, searching the flat for clues, alerting Chief Holgersson and forensics man Nyberg, and blotting out their personal feelings as best they can. A shotgun lies on the floor and Wallander tells Holgersson grimly: 'Murder or suicide, I don't know which.' Nyberg arrives without knowing it is his friend Svedberg who has been killed. He is shocked but insists that from the position of the shotgun, it is murder they must investigate, not suicide. Wallander is relieved to learn that Svedberg did not take his own life. He is determined to find the killer as soon as possible but there are no obvious clues. None of the neighbours seem to have seen or heard anything and no one knows more than the slightest detail about Svedberg's private life. He lived alone and, apart from interests in American Indians and astronomy, he seemed to devote all his time to his job as a policeman. Svedberg had been involved with trying to track down the missing youngsters before anyone, apart from the one anxious mother, seriously suspected anything terrible had happened to them. Chief Holgersson invites Svedberg's closest colleagues to lunch at her home where she and Wallander speak about their memories of their murdered friend. Wallander tells everyone how Svedberg joined the police because he believed it would help to cure his fear of the dark, which he had suffered from ever since he was a young child. Svedberg had never been able to understand or overcome this fear and joining the police had made no difference at all. He used to sleep with the light on at night because he hated the darkness so much.

Wallander goes to interview one of Svedberg's two living relatives and finds himself talking to a strange man, a professor who studies man's relationships with monsters and who also works as a consultant to American film companies. He is very eccentric and clearly very rich. Mankell's ability to come up with interesting characters seems to never flag. The professor lives in an extraordinary house, which Wallander is astonished to discover Svedberg regularly looked after for him when he was travelling abroad. And the detective is even more amazed when the professor explains that Svedberg used to bring his girlfriend whenever he was staying. Wallander had no idea Svedberg had a woman in his life. He had always appeared to be the ultimate confirmed bachelor, devoted to his job and interested in Red Indians and astronomy, but not remotely taken with the opposite sex. This sounds like a possible lead at last but all the professor knows about Svedberg's lady friend is that her first name is Louise. He explains: 'Our family is not one for idle curiosity.' The only things he is able to add is that Louise changed her hair colour pretty frequently (he found a series of different coloured hairs in the bathroom) and that he thinks Svedberg was very much in love with her.

Wallander is stunned. Svedberg might only have been dead for a couple of days but they already know much more about him than when he was alive.

Wallander forgets that he has arranged to meet his old friend, Sten Widen, until he is reminded by a phone call from Widen. Wallander apologises and blames work for distracting him. He asks Widen to wait and rushes to his house to see him. They reminisce about old times and, at one point, Widen removes a piece of wood panelling to find a photograph he is anxious to show Wallander. The men get on well and enjoy some whisky together. Wallander eventually gets a taxi home and goes to sleep in the back. He slips into a dream but then he is suddenly awakened by a thought. Widen has put an idea of hidden compartments into his mind and he realises that Svedberg might have a hidden compartment in his flat that they have not yet found. In spite of the large amount of whisky he has drunk, he gets the taxi driver to divert to take him back to Svedberg's place. It is the early hours of the morning. Wallander still has Svedberg's keys in his pocket and he enters the flat. First he pours himself a glass of water and takes some aspirin from Svedberg's medicine cabinet. Then he sets out to find Svedberg's hidden compartment. It takes him just over an hour but eventually he discovers a brown envelope that someone has clearly tried to make secret. Inside the envelope are two photographs. One is a photograph of a woman's face while the other is a picture of a group of young people in old-fashioned costumes. Wallander looks carefully at the photograph and realises after a moment or two that one of the girls in the picture is Astrid Hillstrom, daughter of the outspoken Mrs Hillstrom. Wallander is absolutely astonished. What he had imagined to be two completely separate cases have suddenly collided with a bang. It seems that Svedberg went on a secret one-man investigation into the 'disappearance' of the four youngsters.

As the workload of the detectives increases, so Wallander's ability to eat and drink sensibly decreases. He is totally focussed on the case and keeps thinking that he will put off doing something about his diet and his diabetes until after he discovers the identity of Svedberg's killer. He grabs food on the run wherever and whenever he can. At one point he stops at a café at the bus station and orders a cup of coffee and a sandwich. It is only after his sandwich has arrived that he realises he should have ordered it without butter. Feeling suddenly guilty, he starts to scrape off the butter with his knife and then sees the man at the next table is watching him intently. Wallander's picture has been in the newspapers recently and he realises the man has recognised him. He imagines this will probably lead to rumours about police frittering away their time scraping butter of sandwiches instead of searching for their colleague's killer. He sighs sadly. He has never wanted attention from the public and he feels more than ever under pressure. The job weighs more heavily than usual on his shoulders. His grim view about life as a police officer is hardly improved by a letter from Per Akeson, the former chief prosecutor, who has taken a leave of absence and is working in Uganda for the International Refugee Commission. His daily life seems so dramatic and fascinating that Wallander feels envious. As his fiftieth birthday looms not far ahead, he realises there is unlikely to be an exciting new challenge to take him away from the exhausting grind of police work.

Mankell has many great gifts as a writer of crime thrillers. For this reader the greatest of these is the ability to surprise and totally rivet his readers. Although the shocking killing of three young people starts the book, the passage when the bodies are eventually found – the killer having stored the corpses and then ghoulishly returned them to the locations where they were shot – is equally electrifying. Even a hardened policeman throws up at the sight and you know exactly how he feels. All of a sudden Wallander is hunting for a ruthless serial killer and he and his team feel they are floundering hopelessly for genuine clues to the identity of the fiendishly cruel culprit. To convey his outrage Wallander is allowed a rare major expletive as he looks at the bodies, which are in an advanced state of decomposition, and concedes: 'I've never seen anything so fucking horrible.' He experiences a moment of complete helplessness and desperately wishes his wise old colleague Rydberg was still alive so that he could talk to him. He actually admits to himself that he does not believe he can handle the pressure any longer and starts to think another officer like Martinsson or Hansson will have to take over from him. Wallander feels burnt out and is still poleaxed by the news that he has developed diabetes. He feels he is on a downward spiral. But as other officers arrive at the macabre scene and gather round him, Wallander realises he has to stay in charge and try to appear confident even if he doesn't feel it. He knows he is the one who must tell everyone what to do. It is a desperately grim time for him and his team. As the area is searched and the forensics officer, Nyberg, goes into action, Wallander watches them and knows that just about every member must be wishing they had decided to become anything but a police officer. Three young people have been shot dead just as they were enjoying a historical picnic in the countryside. This is perhaps in some ways the most upsetting case that Wallander has encountered in his long career. He thinks that until now he has never believed anyone is born evil. He has always thought people do terrible things and become evil because of their environments or circumstances. But as he gazes at the three executed young people he senses the actions of a really black and evil mind.

A fourth young person, called Isa Edengren, should have been in the deadly picnic party but she was unwell on the day they were gunned down. She takes an overdose and Wallander finds her just in time and has her rushed to hospital to save her life. It is a very emotional experience that reminds Wallander of the day his daughter Linda tried to commit suicide when she was 15 years old. He later realised that Linda's teenage anguish was just one of a series of triggers that led to his wife Mona walking out on him. Although he and Linda talked about it afterwards he never really understood why his daughter could have felt so desolate that she wanted to end her life. And he can't understand young Isa's reasons either. She had been going to celebrate Midsummer at the picnic and then had not been well enough to go because of a stomach bug. Wallander has the grim job of telling Isa that her friends are dead. Afterwards he thinks to himself that he simply cannot go on having to undertake such distressing tasks. He drives around unable to sleep and goes back to the murder scene in the middle of the night. He remembers another murder, the killing of a young girl some years ago, when they were unable to discover the murderer. That failure had haunted Wallander and his old pal for years afterwards and he wonders if this new case will be as much of a nightmare in years to come.

Just as Wallander is at a low point with the complex and confusing investigation, he gets a message to ring his ex-wife Mona. Fearing that something awful has happened to Linda, he calls straight away. But Mona has news of a different kind. She wants to tell her husband she is getting married again. Wallander is in no mood to be gracious and offer kind words and congratulations. Instead, he sneeringly asks her if she should really be marrying a golfer. Clearly Wallander has not got much time for people who spend their time hitting a little white ball around the countryside. Mona is miffed but Wallander is tired and edgy, and he swears angrily and slams the phone down so hard that it breaks. At that point Martinsson is just walking into his office. Wallander says that his anger is a private matter and Martinsson wisely keeps out of it, though he does say that he will get his boss a new phone. Wallander is still seething and he is once more forced to accept to himself that his feelings for Mona are still there to an extent, even though he knows there is no chance of them getting back together. His doctor keeps pressing him to come in for a full examination but Wallander is determined to devote every waking moment to his investigation. He traces Isa's parents, who are staying in their house in Spain and have no plans to rush back and look after her. Wallander fumes and makes his disapproval of their less than caring attitude abundantly clear.

When Isa goes missing from the hospital, Wallander sets off to search for her in another of the family's properties on a remote island in northern Sweden. He finds her and manages to gain her confidence enough to discover some more of the motivations of the young people dressing up in costume for a picnic in the countryside. They agree to go back in the morning but Isa is shot and killed by a mystery intruder during the night. Wallander is distraught and furious with himself that he has allowed Isa to be killed while he was supposed to be caring for her. On his long drive home he has a happier encounter with a friendly lady café owner, who recognises that he is a policeman in need of sleep and offers him a bed for a few hours. She is divorced from a policeman herself so she spots the signs and there is a tender moment between them before he drives off back to Ystad. Back home, he at last goes to the doctor for a full examination and receives a stern warning that he must start to look after himself better or he could get into serious trouble with his health. Wallander goes through the motions of agreeing to eat and drink more sensibly but he is still strangely ashamed of being diagnosed with diabetes and overwhelmed with the complexity and violence of the killings he is desperately trying to solve. Wallander receives a warning with regard to his health when, midway through a conversation with Martinsson about a possible witness, he suddenly collapses. He soon recovers himself and although an ambulance is called, he gulps down some water and sugar lumps and flatly refuses to go to hospital. The other officers are shocked. Hansson thinks Wallander has had a stroke but he insists on going ahead with the meeting. When they take a break he rings his doctor who is not at all surprised. He tells Wallander his blood-sugar level will continue to go up and down until he is properly assessed and they get his treatment fixed.

Wallander refuses to worry about his health and he also refuses to admit to anyone that he has diabetes. He has more trouble on his hands from a senior prosecutor called Thurnberg, who is unhappy with the lack of arrests. He tells Wallander he is going write him a detailed assessment of his failings and he expects a speedy written response. Wallander is furious. He tells Thurnberg he can't believe they should be writing letters to each other when a killer, who has already claimed five lives, is on the loose. Wallander bangs the table and shouts at the young bureaucrat who, he decides, can't be more than 33 years old. Ann-Britt sympathises with Wallander but she does not believe him when he insists his health is fine. Thurnberg feels seriously insulted and wants to remove Wallander from the investigation. But before the disagreement can progress any further there is terrible news. A newly-wed couple are shot dead on a beach together with their photographer and the assassin has got clean away. With eight people dead, the pressure to get a result really builds on the police. Martinsson begins to waver and starts to doubt the point of even being a policeman. He is upset and horrified that his young son wants to follow him into the job. Wallander offers to talk to the boy to try to explain what it is really like to work as a policeman.

The police get a promising lead when the woman in the photograph found in Svedberg's flat is located in a bar in Malmö. Wallander rushes over and introduces himself. The woman says she's happy to talk to him, once she has been to the toilet. Wallander waits but she doesn't come back out. It seems she has sneaked out another way and Wallander feels less like an ace detective than ever. Only men have come out of the toilet area and Wallander realises that the woman must have somehow disguised herself as a man to make her escape. He feels like an idiot. Back in Ystad he faces another meeting with flagging, disillusioned colleagues whom he knows he is going to further disappoint by revealing his error in letting the woman slip through his grasp. Wallander is very down as the investigation seems to be stalling, but he is definitely not out and is still full of enough energy to speak sharply to Martinsson. They are discussing the possibility that Svedberg might have been homosexual and they are trying to consider if he'd had a relationship with a certain suspect. Martinsson says the man might have had 'deviant tendencies' and Wallander delivers a quick lecture. He says: 'In this day and age homosexuality can hardly be regarded as deviant. Maybe in the 1950s, but not now. That people might still want to conceal their sexual preferences is another matter entirely.' This is a much more modern, politically-correct Wallander than the man most readers would recognise from earlier novels. Mankell is clearly making Wallander change to keep up with changing attitudes.

More trouble for Wallander looms when the parents of the murdered youngsters go to the newspapers to complain that the police in general, and Wallander in particular, have not done enough to protect their offspring. Wallander is given the chance to comment but chooses not to. He is also facing a complaint from a jogger who had run onto the original murder scene and been sent away with a flea in his ear by Wallander. Much more dangerously, Mankell lets us know that the killer is now targeting Wallander himself.

The final showdown is chilling and it shows Wallander at his most human, forgetting both his gun and his mobile phone. He heads home only to find the killer hiding in his flat, waiting to execute him. Wallander has worked out that as the villain realised the net was finally tightening around him, he would go for one final target. He just hadn't quite calculated that it was him. No one can accuse Wallander of behaving like a superhero. When his final pursuit of the murderer becomes a car chase, he discovers he's almost out of petrol. But without wishing to give away every detail it will surprise no one to discover that Wallander finally gets his man, or possibly woman in the case of this curious, sex-changing, psychopath who murdered people simply for being happy.

In conclusion, after a brief period to recover from his injuries and attempt to get his diabetes and high blood pressure under control, Wallander is faced by yet another challenge. He has promised Martinsson that he will talk to his 11-year-old son, David, about his ambitions to follow his father into the police force. After developing diabetes and surviving a singularly traumatic murder investigation, Wallander is signed off on sick leave. The schoolboy peppers Wallander with a series of very probing, direct questions about his own ambitions at the start of his career. Wallander tries to be as honest as he can when he answers the boy. He tells David his own father was against him becoming a policeman and never came to terms with it. He advises David to take his time making his decision and the boy finishes by asking a last question: 'Are you ever scared?' Wallander admits that he is sometimes terrified but that he tries to deal with his fears by thinking about other things.

Ann-Britt is surprised to see Wallander in the office and she wants to tell him some news of her own. Wallander thinks she is about to quit the police and he would hardly blame her, though she would be a huge loss. But in fact what she wants to tell him is that she is getting a divorce. Wallander sympathises but Ann-Britt has more news. The serial killer that Wallander risked his life to capture is writing a book about his murders and has probably already agreed a large advance from the publishers. The killer reveals to Wallander that he shot Svedberg, who had become his lover, because he had discovered his secret.

Wallander knows he will never forget his long interviews with the crazy killer who murdered people for being happy. It transpires that he was badly treated as a child and, after he was sacked from his job, had somehow become bizarrely convinced that all smiling people were evil and needed to be exterminated. Wallander is concerned that this sort of rejection in the thrustingly competitive Swedish society might be forcing more people to the margins with bitter grudges against humanity. The thought sickens him. He worries that the steady growth in the use of violence during his lifetime means that they are heading for a complete breakdown of society, an idea that chills him to the bone. So far as his health problems go, Wallander is at last dealing with his diabetes and high blood pressure. He is finally following doctor's orders.

One Step Behind was published in Sweden in 1997 and was first published in Great Britain in 2002. BBC Radio journalist Mark Lawson is a devoted fan of the *Wallander* books and he explained his enthusiasm in a review of *One Step Behind* in the *Guardian*: 'Why is *One Step Behind* so compelling that, at the end of the sleepless night it took to read, I blearily reached for a keyboard to web-search for Mankell's other titles in translation? The answer, I think, is that, while the sleuth slightly less ruined than the world he inhabits is a familiar protagonist, Wallander has an unusual physical and psychological complexity. He feels like a real man living and, in this book, nearly dying and his final, exhausted heroism as his veins ache has the weight of a small but profound goodness.'

CHAPTER ELEVEN:
FIREWALL

Kurt Wallander is almost 55 as *Firewall* begins. His health is much improved due to his reluctant decision to follow his doctor's advice, rather than simply listening to it and then ignoring most of the instructions. He stays well away from his favourite fast-food places, eats more sensibly and exercises regularly, taking a long walk at least four times a week. His cheeks are looking a little hollow again he is happy to see, instead of the puffed-up face that always used to stare back from the mirror asking: 'Why are you overweight?' It is more than a year since he last spoke to one-time Latvian lover Baiba and she told him she did not want to come and live in Sweden and be his wife. She had a job as a translator and, although it was badly paid, it was rewarding in other ways. She had a life of her own in Latvia whereas in Sweden she realised she would just be Wallander's wife, and that was not enough.

As the book opens, Wallander is going to attend the funeral of Stefan Fredman, the young boy who became an Indian warrior to kill his own brutal, bullying father and the sleazy old men who used and abused his sister. Since his crimes were uncovered in *Sidetracked*, Stefan has been incarcerated in a psychiatric ward. But his tragic life has ended is a suitably horrific manner. He has leapt to his death from a high window in the hospital with full Indian warrior war paint covering his face. Now Stefan's long-suffering mother, Anette, wants Wallander, as the man who finally brought her son's killing spree to an end, to come to the funeral and, although he dislikes funerals intensely, he cannot find it in his heart to refuse. After the service a press photographer upsets Stefan's mother by snatching a picture as they leave the church. Wallander grabs the camera and then removes and ruins the film as the photographer protests angrily. It is a depressing time for Wallander as he notes that Anette is drinking heavily and Stefan's little brother is clearly at risk. But when he gets back to the office he is greeted by a case that seems to mark an even more disturbing decline in Swedish behaviour. Two young girls, one 19 and the other just 14, have assaulted a taxi driver with a hammer and a knife to rob him of his paltry takings. They hit him on the head with the hammer and stabbed him in the chest with the knife, and their excuse is simply that they 'needed money'. Wallander cannot believe the behaviour. Neither girl had been in trouble before and neither of them shows any sign of remorse. Wallander is saddened by the experience of interviewing them both and asks

Martinsson: 'What's happening to the world?' Both men know that the girls are withholding some information about this bizarre attack and Wallander, in particular, is determined to get to the truth. That is a vow that becomes even more fervently held when the news comes through that the taxi driver has died from his injuries. The girls could now face murder charges.

Wallander is living much more sensibly now. Instead of pizzas or hamburgers for every meal, he is attempting to eat healthily as often as possible. He even cuts up vegetables to make his own vegetable soup. But his mood remains largely morose, partly because he is lonely and unhappy that he does not see enough of his daughter Linda. He worries endlessly about where she gets to all the time as she is always out somewhere when he calls. He rings to invite her to come over to Ystad and visit him but again she is not at home. When she rings back next day it is with some advice for her father. But first she wants to know if he has had any contact with Baiba. Wallander says she knows perfectly well that relationship is all over.

Linda tells her father firmly that it is no good for him carrying on living such a solitary life. She accuses him of sounding 'whiny' and suggests he contacts a dating agency to meet a new woman to brighten up his loneliness. Linda says: 'Otherwise you're going to turn into a whiny old man who worries about where I'm spending my nights.' Wallander says he is fine as he is and then realises that his daughter sees right through him as usual, but he flatly refuses to put an advert in a paper searching for a companion. He says he does not believe in such things.

Linda tells her father she is at work at the restaurant so at least he knows where she is for once. It frustrates him to know so little about where she goes or who she sees. But he feels jealous that she has people in her life. In fact, he has already thought of signing up to a dating agency and has almost done so once or twice, but always bottled out at the last minute. He feels that it makes him look too desperate but he is starting to realise that perhaps he is desperate! Wallander goes to visit the family of one of the girls who attacked and killed the taxi driver. He is surprised to find the girl's stepfather is an old friend. He has changed his surname to that of his wife, so Wallander could hardly have known who to expect. But it does not help him gain any insight into the girl's shocking behaviour. He searches her room but finds nothing to throw any light on why she should attack a taxi driver with a hammer. When Wallander gets back to the police station, the new receptionist Irene (who has replaced faithful, kind-hearted and now retired Ebba) tells him that everyone is looking for him as he has forgotten to take his mobile phone with him again. Wallander is irritated and demands to know what she means by 'everyone'. It turns out that Irene is not exaggerating. There has been a general call out for him as Sonja, the older girl who had wielded the hammer, has somehow escaped from police custody. Apparently she asked to go to the toilet and when the officer in charge of her turned his back, she simply walked the other way. No one noticed or even tried to stop her and she walked straight out of the police station. Wallander is furious and Holgersson is also very angry, saying it is 'completely unacceptable'.

Wallander interviews Eva – the other, younger girl – to try to find out where Sonja might have gone. He is shocked to see that Eva looks as if she is still a child. She only seems to be about 12 yet she is accused of stabbing to death a taxi driver. Because of her age, her mother is with her. Wallander tries to talk tough to Eva and he raises his voice and tells her that he doesn't want to hear any lies. She furiously retorts: 'What the fuck are you screaming at me for, you old bastard?' Wallander is taken aback and realises he is more annoyed by being called 'old' than being referred to as a 'bastard', but he still attempts to interrogate the young killer. Wallander turns to the mother to ask her about Sonja but she says simply that she never liked her. This seems to enrage Eva and she swings round and hits her mother in the face, then bites Wallander's hand as he attempts to separate them. Eva yells: 'Get rid of the old hag!' Wallander loses his temper and slaps Eva hard across the face. She is knocked to the floor and Wallander storms out of the room with his hand still stinging from the blow. Holgersson is walking along the corridor and she demands to know what is happening but neither of them sees the journalist who is arriving for the press conference. He has snapped several pictures of Wallander slapping Eva without anyone else noticing his presence.

Wallander is forced to calm down fast as he is to address the press conference. He goes to the toilet and splashes cold water on his face. He is seething over the altercation with the girl but also angry that he has to talk to journalists about the case. He hates meetings with the media. He used to simply dislike them but now he actively hates them with a passion. He explains to the audience of journalists that two people have confessed to attacking and robbing the taxi driver, who has died from his injuries. But when he adds that one of the attackers has recently escaped from police custody, there is uproar in the room as the journalists demand more information than Wallander is prepared to give them. He is feeling unwell and he brings an abrupt end to the press conference. Chief Holgersson questions what he is doing but he tells her she will have to take charge as he is going home. She is surprised and Wallander tells her she can feel his brow if she wishes, but he is running a temperature and he is going home. He leaves without waiting for her response. He knows that he should stay and sort out the mess but he feels weak and totally without energy. He leaves via the garage to avoid meeting reporters. But when he turns the key, his car refuses to start. He is forced to walk home where he collapses into bed completely exhausted. Next morning he wakes out of a wild dream involving a press conference going completely out of control and his father calmly painting at the back of the room. He feels desperately rough and his throat is swollen but his temperature does seem to have gone down. He makes himself some tea and rings the police station to get up to date. He is disappointed to learn that Sonja has disappeared without a trace.

Still feeling under the weather, Wallander promises to be back at work tomorrow. He lies on the sofa and attempts to console himself with a CD of Verdi's *La Traviata*. He closes his eyes and considers angry Eva and her sudden attack on her mother. His peace is interrupted by a phone call. It is Sten Widen, one of Wallander's very few friends, ringing with momentous news. He has called to say goodbye. He has finally sold the ailing stud farm that he inherited from his father and is about to fulfil a long held dream of leaving Sweden to start a brand new life. Wallander is instantly jealous and asks where his friend is heading, only to be told that he has yet to make up his mind. Wallander promises to come over and visit his friend before he leaves for his new life. He puts the phone down and is left feeling full of envy. His own ambitions to one day do something other than be a police officer in Ystad seem to have vanished into the sunset many years ago. He is beginning to think he will never escape.

All of a sudden, a power cut plunges much of the town into darkness, including Wallander's home in Mariagatan. Electrical engineers go into action to try to find out what has gone wrong and in a substation they make a grisly discovery. A human body has short-circuited the entire region. Hansson and Martinsson collect Wallander on the way to investigate. They are first met by the smell of burnt human flesh and soon afterwards are confronted by another shock. The body is that of escaped taxi-driver-attacker, Sonja. Just as Wallander is attempting to work out how on earth Sonja came to lose her young life in the substation, and decide whether she committed suicide or was cruelly murdered, another shock arrives for the troubled detective. A newspaper splashes the story that a well-known policeman has assaulted a teenage girl and runs a story about Wallander hitting Eva, complete with damning pictures that capture the violence of the moment very vividly. Wallander is astonished. He didn't think anyone else witnessed his reaction to Eva lashing out at her mother. Holgersson guesses correctly that a journalist arrived early for the press conference and snapped the incriminating picture from the corridor.

Wallander feels totally devastated. In his 30-year career he has often been involved in fights and scuffles with suspects during difficult arrests. But he has never hit anyone during an interrogation until he slapped this out-of-control girl. Wallander explains that the girl was attacking her mother and says he lashed out to protect her and to calm the girl down. Holgersson is annoyed that Wallander has not mentioned the incident to her earlier and says she has no alternative but to order an investigation. Wallander is furious as he detects in Holgersson's voice that she does not believe his version of events. And it gets worse when she says the girl and her mother both insist Wallander's slap came out of the blue. He is stunned and reels back with surprise at this allegation. All of a sudden he thinks his career is over. He is devastated and in that moment decides that he will resign from the police force. He storms out of the police station in a cold rage. He knows that he is telling the truth about what happened but he also knows that Holgersson does not believe him. He feels that this leaves him with no alternative. He must resign from the police. He goes out and buys a bottle of whisky and then heads home. If there is one single thing that Wallander cannot bear it is having his word questioned or doubted. He is telling the truth and he is outraged that Holgersson does not believe him. 'Never have a woman for a boss,' he thinks furiously to himself. He does get support from Hansson and from Nyberg, which heartens him. He can tell that they both believe his version of events, which helps to slightly lift his spirits.

Wallander realises he had been wrong to leave the station and go home. He should have stayed at work and fought his ground. He should have talked to every damned journalist who wanted to hear his true version of what happened. He decides that his moment of weakness is over. Now he is starting to get angry. Ann-Britt calls at his house. She clearly wants to hear the truth from the horse's mouth. Wallander tells her what happened and how annoyed he is that Holgersson is not accepting his story as the truth and supporting him. Ann-Britt tries to explain that Holgersson has to listen to all sides and she points out that the pictures in the paper do look bad. Wallander insists again that he did slap the girl but only because she had been laying into her mother. Ann-Britt says she thinks the mother is smart and that she is behind the lies because she sees it as a way to deflect guilt away from her daughter, and now that Sonja is dead they can blame everything about the attack on her. She is the much older girl. Wallander realises it will be his word against theirs.

Wallander is grateful for Ann-Britt's support but he needs something to take his mind off police work altogether. He visits old friend Sten Widen in order to hear his plans for the future. Wallander warns Sten that he must not simply drink himself to death when he gets the money from the sale of the stud. And Wallander reflects grimly that while Sweden was once a haven of sanity in a frightening and uncertain world, it has now become somewhere from where people want to escape. Sten says that he has been considering what to do and his first thought is to become a stage technician. He wants to go to La Scala in Milan to operate the curtain! Wallander points out that this dream might be a little far-fetched and Sten says that he has plenty of alternative ideas. Bleakly, he even says he might go to the north of Sweden and bury himself in the largest snowdrift he can find. All he knows is that the stud is going to be sold so he will have to go somewhere. Wallander tells his friend of his problems dealing with unbalanced young girls who think it is acceptable to kill a taxi driver just because they need some money.

Sten does not understand how Wallander can spend his life dealing with the dregs of society. But Wallander insists he is not a quitter. He believes in the work of the police even though it is often exhausting and frustrating. Wallander realises that although he and Sten were friends when they were young men, there is little between them now and he makes plans to return home early. Wallander knows that in reality their friendship ended a long time ago, though he does make Sten promise to keep him in touch with whatever it is he chooses to do once the stud is sold. Wallander is left with a feeling of vague melancholy. Even though their friendship is long over, he knows he is going to miss Sten. There is no one else around to connect him with his earlier life.

Wallander returns to the police station convinced that Eva somehow knows that Sonja has been murdered and that is what has encouraged her to change her story. He is shocked to be confronted by the journalist who took the incriminating picture. He wants to do an interview. Wallander agrees, so long as a third party is there as a witness and Martinsson is recruited to assist. Holgersson later insists that there will be an internal inquiry into Wallander's alleged assault of Eva. Wallander is angry at Holgersson's apparently open distrust of him. He goes back over the girls' night out before they attacked the taxi driver. He finds a friendly restaurant owner who recalls their visit, and that of a mysterious Chinese man who sat and ate nearby. As if that is not complex enough, the body of a man who was found dead close to a cash machine on the night of the girls' attack disappears from the mortuary. In its place was left a piece of electrical equipment, of the sort that would come from a substation. Wallander reflects that there must be some sort of link between the girls and the death of the man by the cash machine.

Wallander struggles to continue as normal but the threat of an inquiry into his 'assault' of the young girl hangs heavily over him. He is particularly bitter about Holgersson's lack of support but he is slightly buoyed up when Martinsson insists that he believes his version of what happened. Wallander replies that he has made his mind up, if they try to 'pin' it on him he will resign. He is surprised when he hears himself saying that, but Martinsson says that in that scenario their positions will be reversed from the time when Wallander persuaded Martinsson not to let an unpleasant attack on his daughter make him give up his career. Martinsson says if necessary he will attempt to convince Wallander to stay but Wallander says that he will never be able to persuade him to remain in the police if his mind is made up to leave.

It is a struggle at times for Wallander to keep up his concentration on the investigation. He can't work out if there is a connection between the missing corpse and the dead taxi driver, and he is still troubled by the ongoing investigation into his slapping of Eva. The newspapers are keen to record every detail of his discomfort and he finds himself reading more nonsense than is normal. In fact, he notices in the personal ads there is a woman describing herself as aged 50, divorced and lonely now that her children have grown up. She lists her interests as travel and classical music. Wallander tries to imagine what she might look like but only comes up with a version of Erika, the café-owning ex-wife of another policeman who had kindly given him a place to crash when he was exhausted during *One Step Behind*. He hurls the paper into the newspaper bin but a moment later fishes it out and tears off the page with the personal ads, pushing it into his drawer.

This *Wallander* novel does paint a somewhat sadder picture of a more world-weary man, but our hero does still manage to find the occasional moment of humour. As he is under pressure from the police authorities while the internal investigation is going on, he reacts with a rare joke. Martinsson is going with him to see the widow of the mysteriously missing dead man and he asks if Wallander wishes to walk or take the car. Wallander says he prefers to take the car as he has a hole in his shoe. Martinsson smiles and says: 'What would the national Chief of Police say about that?' Wallander replies: 'We've already put in train his community policing ideas. Why not expand them to include barefoot policing?' It is not the greatest joke ever heard but Wallander is not really in the mood for laughing. He confides in Martinsson that he is very fed-up at having to undergo an inquisition into his conduct. He knows he should have got used to this sort of treatment but he admits he has not. He says that in his long years in the force he has been accused of just about everything, with the possible exception of laziness. He knows he should have developed a thick skin by now but he hasn't.

The idea of finding a lady friend in the personal ads of a newspaper is certainly something that really grabs him. He is not exactly sure that he is such a great catch for any lonely woman and asks himself ruefully if anyone would really be interested in a 50-year-old policeman with diabetes, a cloud over his career and plenty of doubts about his future. He knows that, unlike most people who compile those sorts of adverts, he is not particularly interested in walks in the country, evenings in front of the fire or sailing! Nevertheless, he makes an initial attempt to draft an ad. It reads: '50-year old police officer, divorced, grown-up daughter, tired of being lonely. Appearance and age not important, but you should enjoy the comforts of home and opera.' Then he admits to himself that the ad is not true. Appearance does matter to Wallander and he knows it. He wants someone he can sleep with and who will be a friend and companion for him whenever he wants her, but who will not be a pain in the neck and hanging around when he desires a little of his own space. He attempts a more truthful proposal: '50-year-old police officer, diabetic, divorced, grown-up daughter, wishes to meet someone to spend time with. The woman I'm looking for is attractive, has a good figure and is interested in sex. Send your answer to "Old Dog".' Who would reply to an advert like that, he smiles to himself? No one very balanced, he decides, and turns over to start again. Wallander is interrupted by the arrival in his office of Ann-Britt. Although she knocks on the door, he forgets to remove the personal section of the newspaper and thinks she must realise what he is doing. He immediately becomes irritated and vows never to write a personal ad for real. He thinks he will probably be answered by someone like Ann-Britt, whom he considers is looking very tired at the moment.

Wallander's thoughts are brought dramatically back to the job when he visits the dead man's flat and someone tries to kill him. Some sort of survival instinct alerts Wallander at the last minute and he pulls back from the door before a bullet is fired into the space he has just vacated. The bullet actually tears a small hole in his jacket but misses its intended target. Wallander jerks backwards and trips on the rug, which is what saves his life. He thinks back to the time he was stabbed as a young policeman in Malmö, when the blade of the knife went within ten centimetres of his heart. That evening he measures the distance from the hole in his jacket to where he imagines his heart to be. It is nine centimetres and he reflects that his margin for survival has decreased over 30 years by just a centimetre. The gunman vanishes without trace.

The plot really thickens when the dead man's body is returned, stark naked but with two of his fingers sliced off, to the spot where he fell, close to the cash machine. Wallander's main hope for information is centred on the dead man's assistant; an attractive woman who is clearly amused by the detective's strange interviewing technique. He telephones in the middle of the night and warns her that some of his questions might appear a little odd. The woman laughs and says that she finds everything about him a little odd. Slowly Wallander realises he is on the fringe of a potentially massive crime involving computer wizards. He himself is particularly useless when it comes to any sort of cutting-edge technology so calls in an ace hacker, who was recently convicted of getting inside the Pentagon's computer system, to help the investigation.

In a lonely moment soon afterwards, Wallander

somehow forgets his vow to forget all about the internet dating idea. He notices an advert for a firm called 'Computerdate' and idly sketches out an application. His heart is only half in it but all the same he feels it is now or never. He is embarrassed about having to go to such measures to find a partner in life but he consoles himself that no one will ever know. He decides to go for the direct approach and swiftly taps out: 'Policeman, divorced, one child, seeking companionship. Not marriage, but love.' He gives himself the name 'Labrador', which sounds a little more promising than 'Old Dog'. He saves his application on his computer, prints out a copy and puts it in an envelope. Privately, he realises he is feeling quite excited about the prospect of getting a new lady in his life though he tells himself he won't get any replies at all.

The investigation broadens dramatically until Wallander and his team are taking on an international gang that uses their skill with computers and the electricity supply chain to create a monumental surge in power that could cripple systems all over the world, leaving the crooks free to step in and benefit from the havoc. But for Wallander, the internal investigation into the slapping of the girl Eva still hangs ominously over him. As long days of difficult and dangerous work go by, Wallander is further disturbed when he discovers that close colleague Martinsson believes he is guilty. Wallander is outraged when Martinsson says carelessly that it is too bad when 'things like this' happen. Wallander picks up the assumption of his guilt instantly and is furious. He demands to know what Martinsson means. The hapless detective tries to excuse himself and says: 'Isn't that what we're always afraid of? That we're going to lose control and start lashing out at people?' Wallander snaps back angrily: 'I slapped her. End of story. I did it to protect her mother.' But he knows that Martinsson does not believe him. Wallander realises that the truth is that probably no one believes him. The picture was so damning and the girl's mother was quick to back up her daughter. Wallander feels totally betrayed and abandoned by his closest colleagues and he knows if they do not support him, then people who do not even know him are hardly likely to fight his corner. He sits in his car feeling completely flat. He is so low he resolves to go and resign his job in the morning. 'Then they can shove this whole investigation up their backsides,' he thinks angrily.

Wallander is still in his black mood when he gets a call to say their tame computer hacker has cracked the villains' system and discovered they have penetrated both the Pentagon and the headquarters of the World Bank. The momentous nature of the investigation he is controlling is in massive contrast to Wallander's activities when he finally gets home and reads the first answer to his personal ad. He gets a reply from a lady called Elvira. She does not include a photograph but Wallander concludes optimistically that she must be very beautiful. Her handwriting is certainly elegant. The dating agency has forwarded his ad and she says she found it interesting. She is 39 years old and divorced. She writes a short letter, which includes her telephone number. At first Wallander is thrilled and almost rings her straight away. Then his more pessimistic side takes over and he becomes convinced that any chance of happiness with Elvira is almost certainly doomed and he is tempted to throw the letter away. He knows he has no time at the moment to even consider a relationship with a woman. The investigation is draining and demanding and takes up literally all of his waking time. He tears up Elvira's letter into small pieces and throws it into the bin. This is an action he very quickly regrets. He resolves to throw himself 100 per cent back into the investigation but then he gets a call to see Chief Holgersson.

Under normal circumstances he enjoys talking to Lisa Holgersson but since she revealed that she does not trust his story over the slapping of Eva, his attitude to her has changed. Holgersson does not beat about the bush and tells him that the investigation into allegations made against him by Eva and her mother is now under way. Wallander wants to know who is in charge of the investigation and Holgersson tells him: 'A man from Hassleholm.' Wallander refuses to be serious and says flippantly: 'A man from Hassleholm? That sounds like the name of a bad television series.' Holgersson warns Wallander that the man is a highly regarded officer and that the Justice Department ombudsman has also had a report of the allegations. And not only him, Holgersson says with feeling before explaining that she has also been reported because she is responsible for the conduct of her officers. Wallander is absolutely furious and gets up to leave. Holgersson says she has not finished and admits it is a difficult situation. Wallander tells Holgersson straight that he is angry that she does not believe his account of what happened. She says that both the girl and her mother say the same thing. Wallander furiously tells his boss that 100 people could say the same thing and he would still be telling the truth. Holgersson refuses to back down and tells Wallander that she is suspending him for as long as the investigation is taking place.

Wallander suddenly becomes very calm. He tells Holgersson that she can do whatever she wants but if she suspends him then he will immediately resign. Holgersson says that sounds like a threat and the two are deadlocked. Wallander says he has been a police officer for a very long time and he knows perfectly well that it is not in the regulations that he has to be suspended. He says that means there is someone higher up who wants an example made of him and she is choosing to go along with that. She admits she was considering finishing the week without any suspension but Wallander says that she must either suspend him now or not do it at all. Holgersson backs down and tells Wallander that he is not suspended but the relationship between them is strained almost beyond belief. Wallander leaves the meeting covered in sweat. He wants nothing more than to write out his resignation and walk out of the police station for good. He cannot believe his boss does not believe in him. But he knows that if he leaves now it will look as if he is guilty. He decides to carry on working but to inform his colleagues of the situation.

Later he goes home and retrieves the pieces of Elvira's letter from the bin. He knows that he does not have a very good reason for doing that but part of the reason is that she has nothing to do with the police. He later rings her and they agree to meet that night in a bar in Malmö, where she lives. When he gets there he finds that she is not hard to pick out, as she is the only woman in the place. Since he was a child Wallander has had the idea that he looks better in profile, so he tries to sit sideways on to Elvira, which feels a little awkward. Wallander is nervous and blurts out more details of his marriage to Mona and their divorce and of his relationship with Baiba than he ever meant to divulge. But Elvira is very easy to talk to and she has a similarly unhappy personal history which she quickly shares with him. She says her second husband was Argentinean but she has not seen him for two years. She and Wallander get on well and chat happily until around 11.30 pm. She insists on splitting the bill and they agree to meet again before heading off in separate directions. Back at his flat alone, Wallander feels as happy as he has been for a long time and goes to bed without even thinking about the case.

Next morning at the police station, Ann-Britt does not take long to wipe the smile off Wallander's face as she tells him she thinks that he should not trust Martinsson too much. She says he is in with Holgersson, going behind his back and criticising what he regards as weak leadership and incorrect priorities. She says it was Martinsson who suggested to Holgersson that he should be suspended. Wallander is furious and asks Ann-Britt if she agrees. She says that if she did, she would tell him to his face. She warns Wallander not to rush in and confront Martinsson straight away but to be warned not to trust him too much.

Wallander has a second date with Elvira, which is interrupted when his computer expert arrives to announce that he has made something of a breakthrough. Wallander is happy for him to speak freely in front of Elvira, which turns out to be a big mistake because the reader finds out very soon, if they have not already tumbled on to her treachery by themselves, that she is working for the gang of ruthless international villains who are preparing a fiendishly clever computer crime to destabilise the financial markets of the whole world. The final pages of *Firewall* are stunningly tense and complex, and the impact on Wallander is enormous. He uses Elvira's place as a safe house for the police computer wizard, which turns out to be an investigative own goal of epic proportions. Not only that, Wallander finds that his life has been put in danger by Martinsson not providing back-up. Martinsson then lies that he was told to stay where he was by Wallander. That is just too much for Wallander to bear and he smashes Martinsson in the face.

Considering the book was written in 1996, the references to the collapse of the world's financial markets are extraordinarily prescient. The whole tone of the final chapters of *Firewall* still feel as up-to-date as tomorrow's newspapers. There is a sensational race against time after Wallander finally discovers which side Elvira is on.

Afterwards, the charges against Wallander for assaulting Eva are dropped when Ann-Britt makes a visit to the girl and her mother. She applies what she calls a 'mild form of emotional blackmail' to mother and daughter and they agree that Wallander's version of events is correct. At the end of the book Wallander is exhausted. Personally and professionally he is vindicated and all thoughts of him being suspended or resigning from the force are over. He realises that the new world of technological crimes is not one where he is happiest. He has become an old dog to whom it is not possible to teach new tricks. But he looks forward to perhaps ten more years as a brilliantly intuitive detective with confidence. He might have to lean on younger brains at times but he knows and believes that his sort of experience is priceless. The energy is still there and, although his relationship with Martinsson is shattered and he was cruelly deceived by evil Elvira, he flatly refuses to give up on his career. He receives a phone call from Baiba that lifts his spirits though perhaps they both know that their relationship is over. He also completes a deal to buy a new car – a Peugeot is what he always drives in print.

But the finale to the book contains a last surprise. Linda shocks her father with the news that she is going to become a policewoman. Wallander thinks about it for a moment and then gives his daughter his blessing. He tells her she can be just the sort of police officer they are going to need in the future.

Firewall was published in Sweden in 1998. It was translated into English and published in 2002. In April

FIREWALL

2004 Stephen Robinson provided this perceptive opinion of the book in the *Daily Telegraph*: 'British devotees of Henning Mankell's Kurt Wallander thrillers have long complained that the series is translated out of sequence so that it is difficult for English speakers to keep proper track of the inspector's progress. In *Firewall*, which came out in Sweden in 1998 and only now is published over here, Wallander is about to turn 50 and suffers from diabetes as well as a profoundly Swedish world-weariness... *Firewall* begins with a series of brutal and apparently random murders. A healthy man falls over dead after using a cash machine. Wallander and his colleagues are scandalised by the premeditated murder of a taxi driver by two teenage girls. One of the girls escapes from custody and is later found electrocuted at an electricity sub-station... The spasm of violence seems random and inexplicable, until Wallander uncovers a plot by a group of cyber-terrorists intent on destroying the global financial system. He turns to a young computer geek, who served time for hacking into the Pentagon's mainframe, to break through the computer firewall masking the cyber-terrorists' conspiracy. In truth, it is an outlandish plot, which Mankell does not deliver wholly successfully. Published seven years ago, *Firewall* nods at the panic of the late 1990s about the Millennium Bug, which seems rather old hat now. But as usual with Mankell's series, the plot is almost incidental to the overall appeal of the book. Kurt Wallander is not a brilliant sleuth, but a dutiful, old-fashioned detective. He is an ordinary man, concerned about his advancing years, and quietly perturbed by the erosion of stolid Scandinavian values in the modern world. Don't read *Firewall* for a dazzling treatment of the threat of cyber-terrorism. But do relish it for the much greater appeal of an original fictional creation whose foibles are so human and recognisable.'

CHAPTER TWELVE:
CONCLUSION

Raymond Chandler said that Dashiell Hammett was the crime writer who: 'Took murder out of the Venetian vase and dropped it in the alley, giving murder back to the kind of people that commit it for a reason, not just to provide a corpse. They do it with the means at hand, not hand-wrought duelling pistols, curare and tropical fish.'

The crucial importance of realism in crime fiction is something upon which Mankell would agree with the great writers of the past. Kurt Wallander will certainly find a place one day in the same great detectives' hall of fame as Sherlock Holmes, Phillip Marlowe, Sam Spade and Inspector Morse.

After *Firewall*, Mankell's eighth *Wallander* novel, was published in 1998 many people considered Sweden's seriously stressed sleuth had closed his last case. Two years later Mankell published *The Return of the Dancing*

Master, which introduced a new police detective, Stefan Lindman, who was based in the small Swedish town of Boras. Like Wallander, Lindman's female partner had walked out on him and like Wallander he had searched for a replacement on an internet dating network. Lindman had other similarities to our hero and in the course of the novel he found himself up against the growing neo-Nazi movement as he investigated the death of a retired police officer.

It was competent rather than compelling and the vital Wallander factor was greatly missed by many readers. Next came Mankell's ingenious attempt to have headstrong Linda Wallander take over the reins of the family detection obsession in *Before The Frost*, published in Sweden in 2002.

It is a fascinating novel, which again sees Mankell using real-life events to form the foundation of his story. The book opens with a prologue introducing a survivor of the 1978 mass suicide in Jonestown, Guyana, becoming involved with a series of bizarre crimes in Ystad that completely bewilder all of the police, including Kurt Wallander. This is where the famous flaming swans come in. A man pours petrol over some swans he has been feeding and then sets them alight. The chilling passage paints a picture that stays in the mind for a long time: 'The burning petrol caught one swan and then all of them. In their agony, their wings on fire, they tried to fly away over the lake, but one by one plunged into the water like fireballs... their dying screams sound like broken trumpets.'

CONCLUSION

Wallander struggles to investigate the bizarre incident, which turns out to be some kind of sacrifice, while his daughter Linda, frustrated at a delay over her starting date as a rookie policewoman, finds herself shocked when her old friend Anna suddenly disappears. After some masterful Mankell magic the two storylines become entwined and Linda takes over as the central character in the book. As the story gets under way, Linda is staying with her father in his small flat in Ystad, which not surprisingly causes problems as well as setting up some tender moments between them. Wallander tells his daughter that he has finally realised that his father probably did not genuinely disapprove of his own decision to become a policeman. Wallander has worked out that his constant disapproval was really a game his father played simply to keep him on his toes. Linda asks if he really believes that and Wallander replies: 'No-one knew him better than I did. I think I'm right. He was a scoundrel through and through. Wonderful, but a scoundrel.'

We also learn that as a teenager Linda made two suicide attempts, not just one as her father thinks. After the wrist-cutting incident she was again gripped by an agonising depression and climbed a bridge, determined to end it all. A policewoman called Annika talked her down and kept her promise never to tell anyone about what had happened. Linda was 16 when she suffered this second crisis and many times she considered telephoning the Malmö police to thank Annika for saving her life, but she had never made the call.

Kurt Wallander is on the edge of the story all the time in *Before the Frost*, but we do find out that he hears from Baiba Leipa in Latvia that she has found another man. Wallander tells his daughter Baiba has fallen in love with a German engineer called Herman, who works at the municipal waterworks in Riga. 'I'm surprised it doesn't drive me insane with jealousy,' he says laconically.

As the two investigations converge, Linda is forced to grow up fast as the sight of a severed head is enough to disturb even the strongest police stomach. Wallander tries to protect his daughter from this grisliest of discoveries but they both soon accept that it is not possible. Linda is just as wilful and determined to ignore the rules to get at the truth as her father has ever been. In fact, it is fascinating to see her inspire in him the same exhortations to be careful as he has produced in colleagues in previous books. At the end of *Before the Frost*, the character of Stefan Lindman, the young policeman from *The Return of the Dancing Master*, has appeared and there is clearly some emotional feeling between him and Linda. And Mankell's ability to weave his story around actual happenings is never better illustrated than by the fact that the events of the novel, which themselves warn darkly of the dangers of fundamentalism, take place just before 11 September 2001. That memorable date is the day Linda formally joins the Ystad police force. She is sitting in the canteen with Martinsson who turns on the television, saying: 'Something's happened in the States.' It must be the gentlest ever reference in print to that terrible day.

CONCLUSION

Before the Frost was a great success but it was not Kurt Wallander's success – it was the launching of Linda that was a triumph. Henning Mankell had planned to write at least three Linda Wallander stories and felt rejuvenated to have a new, younger police officer to carry the narrative. But the tragic death of actress Johanna Sällström, who was such a memorable Linda in the Swedish Wallander films, changed that for good. Henning Mankell was broken-hearted at Sällström's suicide and simply could not bear to carry on writing about Linda as he had intended at the time.

Now there is just one last Kurt Wallander novel for his millions of fans to enjoy. It is to be called *The Troubled Man* in English and will arrive in Great Britain and the United States in 2011. Following the well-trodden path of other *Wallander* works, the book is already published in Scandinavia, Germany and elsewhere on mainland Europe. Mankell has said that this will definitely be the last *Wallander* novel, but added cryptically that his hero does not die. The author explained that he had returned to Wallander, ten years after he had added the prequel collection of stories *The Pyramid*, to give readers the final verdict on the always effective, yet occasionally defective, detective.

Mankell explained his motives at the Edinburgh Book Festival. 'Ten years ago I thought I had finished with Wallander,' he said. 'But after about four or five years I thought maybe there was some story missing about himself.' Mankell realised that the stories had always been about the detective's work more than the man himself, and he resolved to reverse that in the character's final outing. 'It is about Kurt Wallander and what he has learned about life, which is not as much as he thought.'

The final book opens when Hakan von Enke, a retired high-ranking naval officer, disappears during his daily morning walk in the forest outside Stockholm. Wallander's daughter Linda has married von Enke's rich and successful son and is expecting his first grandchild when the disappearance occurs. All of a sudden a family crisis develops extraordinary political implications as the mystery of Von Enke's vanishing becomes linked to Cold War skulduggery involving Soviet submarines in Swedish waters, right wing extremist groups and ruthless hired hitmen. Wallander realises he may have unearthed a dark secret with alarming implications of espionage and betrayal on a large scale.

But by the end of the novel Kurt Wallander, now in his 60s, feels shocked to discover that he may be developing exactly the same the sort of early signs of dementia that his father experienced. The fear that he could be about to go through a similar ordeal to his father's sad decline into Alzheimer's looms large over this dark conclusion to a fantastic detective series. This is not another police procedural but an enthralling climax to a sensational series of books.

Henning Mankell and Kurt Wallander have done as much to bring Sweden into the international limelight as anyone since Abba. Since the day he looked in that Stockholm telephone book for a name for his hero more than 20 years ago, Henning Mankell's *Wallander* stories have sold more than 35 million books in more than 40 countries.

Mankell has blazed the trail for other best-selling Swedish authors like Stieg Larsson and Camilla Läckberg, Norwegian writers like Jo Nesbø and Karin Fossum, and Iceland's Arnalder Indriðason. It seems that readers all over the world have built up an ever-growing appetite in recent years for dark and violent Scandinavian thrillers so long as they're well written

'Twenty-five years ago you had Björn Borg and very few other tennis players in Sweden,' said Mankell. 'Then he had success and then there came Stefan Edberg and Mats Wilander and all of a sudden we had a lot of them. In that way, I might be sort of a locomotive that started the train.'

While *Wallander* in print might be coming to an end, the engine that drives Mankell appears to be as full of life and energy as ever. His charitable work in Africa makes an immense difference to lots of people's lives and his outrage against injustice wherever it occurs burns as fiercely as ever. Mankell sums up his personal philosophy very simply: 'The fundamental driving force for me is to create a change in the world we live in. It is about exploitation, plundering and degradation. I have a small possibility to participate in the resistance. Most of the things that I do are part of a resistance, a form of solidarity work.'

Kurt Wallander is an important part of that resistance. He is a good man forever battling against the odds in a world full of evil. He might have many personal flaws but he is driven on by a shining integrity to do what he can to deliver justice and he will surely be remembered long after all his current readers are long gone.